BY
HEART

AN ANTHOLOGY OF MEMORABLE POEMS

CHOSEN FROM ALL PERIODS BY

FRANCIS MEYNELL

A NONESUCH PRESS CYGNET

M·C·M·L·X·V

Especially for
JANET AND KATE

THE SCOPE OF THIS ANTHOLOGY

This is an unusual and specialised anthology—a collection of memorable poems. They cannot be defined and confined by the word lyric, though melody ("sweet sound" as the mediaevalists interpreted that word) is indeed one of the book's main attributes. For here are poems, English and American, whose directness of communication and whose shape make them fit and even easy to be learnt by heart.

I shall not attempt to make a new definition of poetry in general. No indeed. But I must expand a little on the qualities (directness and shape) that I have looked for.

Directness of communication is essential to memory. The poet's thought and emotion must be at least as clear as an Impressionist painting. You can remember where Monet put his figures and his trees in a favourite picture: it is far harder to remember where an Abstract painter put his colours and angles. This clarity of intent is best if it shows at the first reading of a by-heart poem; it must always be there at a second reading to qualify for this anthology.

By shape I mean that a poem must here have rhyme and rhythm, for these are the two great memory-helps. When one speaks a poem and replaces a forgotten word by a dum, a de-dum, or a dum-de-dum, one pays tribute to the power of rhythm in its most exact form: metre. The help given by rhyme is obvious. But shape must for memory's sake provide also a reasonable brevity, a plain idiom, and the use of friendly and easily spoken words, sometimes bound together by alliteration. Who can forget such a phrase as Shakespeare's "In maiden meditation, fancy-free", with its echoing initial consonants?

My choice of poems has been subject to these conditions and no other. Robert Frost once wrote that no poetry was good for the young that was not equally good for their elders. I heartily agree with him. This collection is planned for people of all ages who have a heart and an ear—the ear is specially important in our context—for poetry. Only in the narrowly limited sense that young people find it easier to memorise than do their elders will BY HEART appeal especially to the young. On the other hand, the no-longer-young will often read here poems they thought they had forgotten, only to find that they can retrieve them almost word for word: an experience that has often been mine as I edited this book.

This, then, is a rhyming and rhythmic selection. The poems have also a simplicity of statement. They simplify thoughts and emotions, sometimes by a revealing compression, sometimes by enlargement and comparison, sometimes even by mere declamation and resonance. This will help them pass one of my simpler and I admit unsociable tests: are they recitable from one's bath? There are other unsociable venues. At the age of eight I was often called upon by my parents to recite the whole thirty-two verses of Gray's "Elegy Written in a Country Churchyard"; and this I invariably did, in shyness, from under the library table. . . . But do not think that by-heart poetry must be recited to others. It is more often for saying, aloud or silently, to oneself. Lord Wavell reports that when he was a small boy an aunt paid him threepence a time for declaiming "Horatius"; but an uncle paid him sixpence for refraining.

While this collection covers all periods, a special feature is the large number of modern, and therefore copyright, poems. This will add much to the reader's interest—as well as to the publisher's costs!—and is the more remarkable and pleasing because so many contemporary poets outlaw themselves from this domain of ours in that they do not *rhyme, or (a lesser number) abjure rhythm, or (and these are not a few) are so private in their meaning that the consequent obscurity must be a barrier to memorising. It is well to remember too that poetry like personality is not always profound because it cannot be understood.*

I have two explanations to make, but the first of them is really a boast. I have made Shakespeare in the glorious poetry of his plays the great exception to my rule-of-rhyme. Shakespeare is after all and all in all the great exception to everything and everybody. I have taken many unrhymed but memory-possessing passages—often no more than single phrases—from the plays.

The second explanation, with a half-apology, is this: I have in a number of cases, and always with intent to preserve the heart of the meaning, chosen passages from long poems difficult because of their length to learn by heart. A signal is always given of these abbreviations: by the word "From" before the title.

During the last war, when London and other cities were being mercilessly bombed, Beatrice Warde wrote a poem which gave a special and commanding reason for learning poetry by heart. I quote one of its three verses:

> Soon you must play your part.
> What are you learning?
> Get it by heart. By heart!
> I have seen books burning.

May the need for that warning never recur. May peace be in the world, and poetry in your heart.

Francis Meynell

Cobbold's Mill
Monks Eleigh, Suffolk
1965

THE ORDER OF CONTENTS

THE 16TH
CENTURY AND
BEFORE

SUMMER IS Y-COMEN IN

Summer is y-comen in!
Loud sing cuckoo!
Groweth seed and bloweth mead,
And springeth the wood new.
Sing cuckoo! cuckoo!

Ewe bleateth after lamb,
Loweth cow after calf;
Bullock starteth, buck verteth;
Merry sing cuckoo!
Cuckoo! cuckoo!
Nor cease thou ever now.
Sing cuckoo now!
Sing cuckoo!

Anonymous

I SING OF A MAIDEN

I sing of a maiden
That is makeless;
King of all kings
To her son she chose.

He came all so still
There his mother was,
As dew in April
That falleth on the grass.

He came all so still
To his mother's bower,
As dew in April
That falleth on the flower.

2—B.H.

He came all so still
There his mother lay,
As dew in April
That falleth on the spray.

Mother and maiden
Was never none but she;
Well may such a lady
God's mother be.

Anonymous

From JOLY JOLY WAT

The shepherd upon a hill he sat;
He had on him his tabard and his hat,
His tarbox, his pipe, and his flagat;
His name was callèd Joly Joly Wat,
For he was a good herdès boy
Ut hoy!
For in his pipe he made so much joy.

The shepherd upon a hill was laid;
His dog to his girdle was tied;
He had not slept but a little braid,
But *Gloria in excelsis* was to him said.
Ut hoy!
For in his pipe he made so much joy.

"Now must I go there Christ was born;
Farewell! I come again to morn.
Dog, keep well my sheep from the corn,
And warn well 'Warroke' when I blow my horn!"
Ut hoy!
For in his pipe he made so much joy.

When Wat to Bethlehem come was,
He sweat, and had gone faster than a pace;
He found Jesu in a simple place,
Between an ox and an ass.
Ut hoy!
For in his pipe he made so much joy.

"Jesu, I offer to thee here my pipe,
My skirt, my tarbox, and my scrip;
Home to my fellows now will I skip,
And also look unto my sheep."
Ut hoy!
For in his pipe he made so much joy.

Anonymous

From TOM OF BEDLAM'S SONG

From the hag and hungry goblin
That into rags would rend ye,
All the spirits that stand
By the naked man
In the book of moons, defend ye.

That of your five sound senses
You never be forsaken,
Nor wander from
Yourselves with Tom
Abroad to beg your bacon.

I slept not since the Conquest,
Till then I never wakèd,
Till the roguish boy
Of love where I lay
Me found and stript me naked.

The moon's my constant mistress,
And the lonely owl my marrow;
The flaming drake
And the night-crow make
Me music to my sorrow.

I know more than Apollo,
For oft, when he lies sleeping,
I see the stars
At mortal wars
In the wounded welkin weeping,

The moon embrace her shepherd,
And the queen of love her warrior,
While the first doth horn
The star of morn,
And the next the heavenly farrier.

With an host of furious fancies,
Whereof I am commander,
With a burning spear
And a horse of air
To the wilderness I wander;

By a knight of ghosts and shadows
I summoned am to tourney
Ten leagues beyond
The wide world's end—
Methinks it is no journey.

Anonymous

THE SPRING

What bird so sings, yet does so wail?
O, 'tis the ravished nightingale!
"Jug, jug, jug, jug, tereu," she cries,
And still her woes at midnight rise.
Brave prick-song! who is't now we hear?
None but the lark so shrill and clear;
Now at heaven's gate she claps her wings,
The morn not waking till she sings.
Hark, hark, with what a pretty throat
Poor robin-redbreast tunes his note;
Hark, how the jolly cuckoos sing!
Cuckoo to welcome in the spring,
Cuckoo to welcome in the spring!

John Lyly

TRUE LOVE

My true-love hath my heart, and I have his,
By just exchange one for another given:
I hold his dear, and mine he cannot miss,
There never was a better bargain driven:
My true-love hath my heart, and I have his.

His heart in me keeps him and me in one,
My heart in him his thoughts and senses guides:
He loves my heart, for once it was his own,
I cherish his because in me it bides:
My true-love hath my heart, and I have his.

Sir Philip Sidney

A FAREWELL TO ARMS

My golden locks Time hath to silver turn'd;
O Time too swift, O swiftness never ceasing!
My youth 'gainst age, and age 'gainst time, hath
   spurn'd,
But spurn'd in vain; youth waneth by increasing:
Beauty, strength, youth, are flowers but fading seen;
Duty, faith, love, are roots, and ever green.

My helmet now shall make an hive for bees,
And lover's sonnets turn to holy psalms;
A man-at-arms must now serve on his knees,
And feed on prayers, which are old age his alms:
But though from court to cottage I depart,
My saint is sure of my unspotted heart.

And when I saddest sit in homely cell,
I'll teach my swains this carol for a song—
"Blest be the hearts that wish my sovereign well,
Curst be the souls that think her any wrong!"
Goddess, allow this agèd man his right
To be your beadsman now that was your knight.

George Peele

From AGINCOURT

Fair stood the wind for France
When we our sails advance,
Nor now to prove our chance
Longer will tarry;
But putting to the main
At Caux, the mouth of Seine,
With all his martial train
Landed King Harry.

And taking many a fort
Furnish'd in warlike sort,
Marcheth tow'rds Agincourt
In happy hour;
Skirmishing day by day
With those that stopp'd his way
Where the French Gen'ral lay
With all his power.

And turning to his men
Quoth our brave Henry then
"Though they to one be ten,
Be not amazèd:
Yet have we well begun;
Battles so bravely won
Have ever to the sun
By fame been raisèd.

"And for myself (quoth he)
This my full rest shall be:
England ne'er mourn for me
Nor more esteem me:
Victor I will remain
Or on this earth lie slain,
Never shall she sustain
Loss to redeem me.

"Poitiers and Cressy tell,
When most their pride did swell,
Under our swords they fell:
No less our skill is

Than when our grandsire great,
Claiming the regal seat,
By many a warlike feat
Lopp'd the French lilies."

The Duke of York so dread
The eager vaward led;
With the main Henry sped
Among his henchmen.
Excester had the rear,
A braver man not there;
O Lord, how hot they were
On the false Frenchmen!

They now to fight are gone,
Armour on armour shone,
Drum now to drum did groan,
To hear was wonder;
That with the cries they make
The very earth did shake;
Trumpet to trumpet spake,
Thunder to thunder.

Well it thine age became,
O noble Erpingham,
Which didst the signal aim
To our hid forces!
When from a meadow by,
Like a storm suddenly
The English archery
Struck the French horses.

With Spanish yew so strong,
Arrows a cloth-yard long,
That like to serpents stung,
Piercing the weather;
None from his fellow starts,
But playing manly parts,
And like true English hearts
Stuck close together.

When down their bows they threw,
And forth their bilboes drew,
And on the French they flew,
No man was tardy;
Arms were from shoulders sent,
Scalps to the teeth were rent,
Down the French peasants went—
Our men were hardy.

Thus while our noble King,
His broad-sword brandishing,
Down the French host did ding,
As to o'erwhelm it;
And many a deep wound lent,
His arms with blood besprent,
And many a cruel dent
Bruisèd his helmet.

Gloster, that Duke so good,
Next of the Royal blood,
For famous England stood
With his brave brother;
Clarence, in steel so bright,
Though but a maiden knight,

Yet in that furious fight
Scarce such another.

Warwick in blood did wade,
Oxford the foe invade,
And cruel slaughter made
Still as they ran up;
Suffolk his axe did ply,
Beaumont and Willoughby
Bare them right doughtily,
Ferrers and Fanhope.

Upon Saint Crispin's day
Fought was this noble fray
Which fame did not delay
To England to carry.
O when shall English men
With such acts fill a pen,
Or England breed again
Such a King Harry!

Michael Drayton

THE PARTING

Since there's no help, come, let us kiss and part,
Nay I have done, you get no more of me;
And I am glad, yea glad with all my heart,
That thus so cleanly I myself can free.

Shake hands for ever, cancel all our vows,
And when we meet at any time again,
Be it not seen in either of our brows
That we one jot of former love retain.

Now at the last gasp of Love's latest breath,
When, his pulse failing, Passion speechless lies,
When Faith is kneeling by his bed of death,
And Innocence is closing up his eyes—

Now if thou would'st, when all have given him over,
From death to life thou might'st him yet recover!

Michael Drayton

THE PASSIONATE SHEPHERD
TO HIS LOVE

Come live with me and be my Love,
And we will all the pleasures prove
That hills and valleys, dale and field,
And all the craggy mountains yield.

There will we sit upon the rocks
And see the shepherds feed their flocks,
By shallow rivers, to whose falls
Melodious birds sing madrigals.

There will I make thee beds of roses
And a thousand fragrant posies,
A cap of flowers, with a kirtle
Embroider'd all with leaves of myrtle.

A gown made of the finest wool,
Which from our pretty lambs we pull,
Fair linèd slippers for the cold,
With buckles of the purest gold.

A belt of straw and ivy buds
With coral clasps and amber studs:

And if these pleasures may thee move,
Come live with me and be my Love.

Thy silver dishes for thy meat
As precious as the gods do eat
Shall on an ivory table be
Prepared each day for thee and me.

The shepherd swains shall dance and sing
For thy delight each May-morning:
If these delights thy mind may move,
Then live with me and be my Love.

Christopher Marlowe

JACK AND JOAN

Jack and Joan they think no ill,
But loving live, and merry still;
Do their week-days' work, and pray
Devoutly on the holy day:
Skip and trip it on the green,
And help to choose the Summer Queen;
Lash out, at a country feast,
Their silver penny with the best.

Well can they judge of nappy ale,
And tell at large a winter tale;
Climb up to the apple loft,
And turn the crabs till they be soft.
Tib is all the father's joy,
And little Tom the mother's boy.
And all their pleasure is Content;
And care, to pay their yearly rent.

Joan can call by name her cows,
And deck her window with green boughs;
She can wreaths and tutties make,
And trim with plums a bridal cake.
Jack knows what brings gain or loss;
And his long flail can stoutly toss:
Makes the hedge, which others break;
And ever thinks what he doth speak.

Now, you courtly dames and knights,
That study only strange delights;
Though you scorn the homespun gray,
And revel in your rich array:
Though your tongues dissemble deep,
And can your heads from danger keep;
Yet, for all your pomp and train,
Securer lives the silly swain.

Thomas Campion

CHERRY-RIPE

There is a garden in her face
Where roses and white lilies grow;
A heavenly paradise is that place,
Wherein all pleasant fruits do flow;
There cherries grow which none may buy,
Till "Cherry-Ripe" themselves do cry.

Those cherries fairly do enclose
Of orient pearl a double row,
Which when her lovely laughter shows,
They look like rose-buds fill'd with snow:
Yet them nor peer nor prince can buy,
Till "Cherry-Ripe" themselves do cry.

Her eyes like angels watch them still;
Her brows like bended bows do stand,
Threat'ning with piercing frowns to kill
All that attempt with eye or hand
Those sacred cherries to come nigh,
—Till "Cherry-Ripe" themselves do cry!

Thomas Campion

SPRING

Spring, the sweet Spring, is the year's pleasant king;
Then blooms each thing, then maids dance in a ring,
Cold doth not sting, the pretty birds do sing,
Cuckoo, jug-jug, pu-we, to-witta-woo!

The palm and may make country houses gay,
Lambs frisk and play, and shepherds pipe all day,
And we hear aye birds tune this merry lay,
Cuckoo, jug-jug, pu-we, to-witta-woo!

The fields breathe sweet, the daisies kiss our feet,
Young lovers meet, old wives a-sunning sit,
In every street these tunes our ears do greet,
Cuckoo, jug-jug, pu-we, to-witta-woo!
Spring! the sweet Spring!

Thomas Nashe

IN TIME OF PESTILENCE

Adieu, farewell earth's bliss!
This world uncertain is:
Fond are life's lustful joys,
Death proves them all but toys.
None from his darts can fly;
I am sick, I must die—
Lord, have mercy on us!

Rich men, trust not in wealth,
Gold cannot buy you health;
Physic himself must fade;
All things to end are made;
The plague full swift goes by;
I am sick, I must die—
Lord, have mercy on us!

Beauty is but a flower
Which wrinkles will devour;
Brightness falls from the air;
Queens have died young and fair;
Dust hath clos'd Helen's eye;
I am sick, I must die—
Lord, have mercy on us!

Strength stoops unto the grave,
Worms feed on Hector brave;
Swords may not fight with fate;
Earth still holds ope her gate;
Come, Come! the bells do cry;
I am sick, I must die—
Lord, have mercy on us!

Wit with his wantonness
Tasteth death's bitterness;
Hell's executioner
Hath no ears for to hear
What vain art can reply;
I am sick, I must die—
Lord, have mercy on us!

Haste therefore each degree
To welcome destiny;
Heaven is our heritage,
Earth but a player's stage.
Mount we unto the sky;
I am sick, I must die—
Lord, have mercy on us!

Thomas Nashe

THE HAPPY HEART

Art thou poor, yet hast thou golden slumbers?
O sweet content!
Art thou rich, yet is thy mind perplexed?
O punishment!
Dost thou laugh to see how fools are vexed
To add to golden numbers, golden numbers?
O sweet content! O sweet, O sweet content!
Work apace, apace, apace, apace;
Honest labour bears a lovely face;
Then hey nonny nonny, hey nonny nonny!

Canst drink the waters of the crispèd spring?
O sweet content!
Swimm'st thou in wealth, yet sink'st in thine own
    tears?
O punishment!

Then he that patiently want's burden bears
No burden bears, but is a king, a king!
O sweet content! O sweet, O sweet content!
Work apace, apace, apace, apace;
Honest labour bears a lovely face;
Then hey nonny nonny, hey nonny nonny!

Thomas Dekker

MATIN SONG

Pack, clouds, away! and welcome, day!
With night we banish sorrow;
Sweet air blow soft, mount lark aloft
To give my Love good-morrow!
Wings from the wind to please her mind
Notes from the lark I'll borrow;
Bird prune thy wing, nightingale sing,
To give my Love good-morrow;
To give my Love good-morrow
Notes from them all I'll borrow.

Wake from thy nest, Robin-red-breast,
Sing birds in every furrow;
And from each bill, let music shrill
Give my fair Love good-morrow!
Blackbird and thrush in every bush,
Stare, linnet, and cock-sparrow,
You pretty elves, amongst yourselves
Sing my fair Love good-morrow!
To give my Love good-morrow
Sing birds in every furrow!

Thomas Heywood

HYMN TO DIANA

Queen and Huntress, chaste and fair,
Now the sun is laid to sleep,
Seated in thy silver chair
State in wonted manner keep:
Hesperus entreats thy light,
Goddess excellently bright.

Earth, let not thy envious shade
Dare itself to interpose;
Cynthia's shining orb was made
Heaven to clear when day did close:
Bless us then with wishèd sight,
Goddess excellently bright.

Lay thy bow of pearl apart
And thy crystal-shining quiver;
Give unto the flying hart
Space to breathe, how short soever:
Thou that mak'st a day of night,
Goddess excellently bright!

Ben Jonson

HAVE YOU SEEN BUT A BRIGHT
LILY GROW

Have you seen but a bright lily grow
Before rude hands have touch'd it?
Have you mark'd but the fall of the snow
Before the soil hath smutch'd it?
Have you felt the wool of beaver,
Or swan's down ever?
Or have smelt o' the bud o' the brier,
Or the nard in the fire?
Or have tasted the bag of the bee?
O so white, O so soft, O so sweet is she!

Ben Jonson

EPITAPH ON DRAKE

Drake, who the world hast conquered like a
    scroll;
Who saw'st the Arctic and the Antarctic Pole;
If men were silent, stars would make thee known:
Phoebus forgets not his companion.

Thomas Beedome

SHAKESPEARE
MAINLY FROM THE PLAYS

SONNET 29

When in disgrace with fortune and men's eyes,
I all alone beweep my outcast state,
And trouble deaf Heaven with my bootless cries,
And look upon myself, and curse my fate,
Wishing me like to one more rich in hope,
Featur'd like him, like him with friends possess'd,
Desiring this man's art, and that man's scope,
With what I most enjoy contented least;
Yet in these thoughts myself almost despising,
Haply I think on thee,—and then my state
(Like to the lark at break of day arising
From sullen earth) sings hymns at heaven's gate;
For thy sweet love remember'd such wealth brings,
That then I scorn to change my state with kings.

SONNET 30

When to the sessions of sweet silent thought
I summon up remembrance of things past,
I sigh the lack of many a thing I sought,
And with old woes new wail my dear time's waste:
Then can I drown an eye, unus'd to flow,
For precious friends hid in death's dateless night,
And weep afresh love's long-since cancell'd woe,
And moan the expense of many a vanish'd sight.
Then can I grieve at grievances foregone,
And heavily from woe to woe tell o'er
The sad account of fore-bemoanèd moan,
Which I new pay as if not paid before.
But if the while I think on thee, dear friend,
All losses are restor'd, and sorrows end.

SONNET 65

Since brass, nor stone, nor earth, nor boundless sea,
But sad mortality o'ersways their power,
How with this rage shall beauty hold a plea,
Whose action is no stronger than a flower?
O, how shall summer's honey breath hold out
Against the wreckful siege of battering days,
When rocks impregnable are not so stout,
Nor gates of steel so strong, but Time decays?
O fearful meditation! where, alack!
Shall Time's best jewel from Time's chest lie hid?
Or what strong hand can hold his swift foot back?
Or who his spoil of beauty can forbid?
O none, unless this miracle have might,
That in black ink my love may still shine bright.

SONNET 66

Tir'd with all these, for restful death I cry,—
As, to behold desert a beggar born,
And needy nothing trimm'd in jollity,
And purest faith unhappily forsworn,
And gilded honour shamefully misplac'd,
And maiden virtue rudely strumpeted,
And right perfection wrongfully disgrac'd,
And strength by limping sway disablèd,
And art made tongue-tied by authority,
And folly (doctor-like) controlling skill,
And simple truth miscall'd simplicity,
And captive good attending captain ill:
Tir'd with all these, from these would I be gone,
Save that, to die, I leave my love alone.

SONNET 94

They that have power to hurt and will do none,
That do not do the thing they most do show,
Who, moving others, are themselves as stone,
Unmovèd, cold, and to temptation slow;
They rightly do inherit Heaven's graces,
And husband nature's riches from expense;
They are the lords and owners of their faces,
Others but stewards of their excellence.
The summer's flower is to the summer sweet
Though to itself it only live and die;
But if that flower with base infection meet,
The basest weed outbraves his dignity:
For sweetest things turn sourest by their deeds:
Lilies that fester smell far worse than weeds.

SONNET 116

Let me not to the marriage of true minds
Admit impediments. Love is not love
Which alters when it alteration finds,
Or bends with the remover to remove:
O no; it is an ever-fixèd mark,
That looks on tempests, and is never shaken;
It is the star to every wandering bark,
Whose worth's unknown, although his height be
    taken.
Love's not Time's fool, though rosy lips and cheeks
Within his bending sickle's compass come;
Love alters not with his brief hours and weeks,
But bears it out even to the edge of doom.
If this be error, and upon me prov'd,
I never writ, nor no man ever lov'd.

SONNET 128

How oft, when thou, my music, music play'st,
Upon that blessèd wood whose motion sounds
With thy sweet fingers, when thou gently sway'st
The wiry concord that mine ear confounds,
Do I envy those jacks that nimble leap
To kiss the tender inward of thy hand,
Whilst my poor lips, which should that harvest reap,
At the wood's boldness by thee blushing stand!
To be so tickled, they would change their state
And situation with those dancing chips,
O'er whom thy fingers walk with gentle gait,
Making dead wood more blest than living lips.
Since saucy jacks so happy are in this,
Give them thy fingers, me thy lips to kiss.

SONNET 146

Poor soul, the centre of my sinful earth,
Fool'd by these rebel powers that thee array,
Why dost thou pine within, and suffer dearth,
Painting thy outward walls so costly gay?
Why so large cost, having so short a lease,
Dost thou upon thy fading mansion spend?
Shall worms, inheritors of this excess,
Eat up thy charge? Is this thy body's end?
Then, soul, live thou upon thy servant's loss,
And let that pine to aggravate thy store;
Buy terms divine in selling hours of dross;
Within be fed, without be rich no more:
So shalt thou feed on Death, that feeds on men,
And, Death once dead, there's no more dying then.

SONG from TWELFTH NIGHT

O Mistress mine, where are you roaming?
O stay and hear! your true-love's coming
That can sing both high and low;
Trip no further, pretty sweeting,
Journeys end in lovers' meeting—
Every wise man's son doth know.

What is love? 'tis not hereafter;
Present mirth hath present laughter;
What's to come is still unsure:
In delay there lies no plenty,—
Then come kiss me, Sweet-and-twenty,
Youth's a stuff will not endure.

SONG from MEASURE
FOR MEASURE

Take, O take those lips away
That so sweetly were forsworn,
And those eyes, the break of day,
Lights that do mislead the morn:
But my kisses bring again,
Bring again—
Seals of love, but sealed in vain,
Sealed in vain!

Hide, O hide those hills of snow,
Which thy frozen bosom bears,
On whose tops the pinks that grow
Are of those that April wears.
But first set my poor heart free
Bound in those icy chains by thee.

SONG from A MIDSUMMER NIGHT'S DREAM

You spotted snakes with double tongue,
Thorny hedgehogs, be not seen;
Newts and blind-worms, do no wrong;
Come not near our fairy queen.
Philomel, with melody,
Sing in our sweet lullaby;
Lulla, lulla, lullaby; lulla, lulla, lullaby!
Never harm
Nor spell nor charm,
Come our lovely lady nigh;
So, good night, with lullaby.

Weaving spiders, come not here;
Hence, you long-legg'd spinners, hence!
Beetles black, approach not near;
Worm nor snail, do no offence.
Philomel, with melody,
Sing in our sweet lullaby;
Lulla, lulla, lullaby; lulla, lulla, lullaby!
Never harm
Nor spell nor charm,
Come our lovely lady nigh;
So, good night, with lullaby.

SONG from THE MERCHANT OF VENICE

Tell me, where is Fancy bred,
Or in the heart, or in the head?
How begot, how nourishèd?
Reply, reply.

It is engender'd in the eyes,
With gazing fed; and Fancy dies
In the cradle where it lies:
Let us all ring Fancy's knell;
I'll begin it,—Ding, dong, bell.
Ding, dong, bell.

SONG from AS YOU LIKE IT

Under the greenwood tree,
Who loves to lie with me,
And tune his merry note
Unto the sweet bird's throat,
Come hither, come hither, come hither;
Here shall he see
No enemy,
But winter and rough weather.

SONG from CYMBELINE

Fear no more the heat o' the sun,
Nor the furious winter's rages;
Thou thy worldly task hast done,
Home art gone, and ta'en thy wages:
Golden lads and girls all must,
As chimney-sweepers, come to dust.

Fear no more the frown o' the great;
Thou art past the tyrant's stroke:
Care no more to clothe and eat;
To thee the reed is as the oak:
The sceptre, learning, physic, must
All follow this, and come to dust.

42

Fear no more the lightning-flash,
Nor the all-dreaded thunder-stone;
Fear not slander, censure rash;
Thou hast finish'd joy and moan:
All lovers young, all lovers must
Consign to thee, and come to dust.

No exorciser harm thee!
Nor no witchcraft charm thee!
Ghost unlaid forbear thee!
Nothing ill come near thee!
Quiet consummation have;
And renownèd be thy grave!

From TWELFTH NIGHT

Viola
Make me a willow cabin at your gate,
And call upon my soul within the house;
Write loyal cantons of contemnèd love,
And sing them loud, even in the dead of night;
Holla your name to the reverberate hills,
And make the babbling gossip of the air
Cry out Olivia! O, you should not rest
Between the elements of air and earth,
But you should pity me.

*

She never told her love,
But let concealment, like a worm i' the bud,
Feed on her damask cheek: she pined in thought;
And, with a green and yellow melancholy,
She sat like patience on a monument,
Smiling at grief. Was not this love, indeed?

From A MIDSUMMER NIGHT'S DREAM

Oberon
That very time I saw,—but thou couldst not,—
Flying between the cold moon and the earth,
Cupid all arm'd: a certain aim he took
At a fair vestal, thronèd by the west;
And loos'd his love-shaft smartly from his bow,
As it should pierce a hundred thousand hearts:
But I might see young Cupid's fiery shaft
Quench'd in the chaste beams of the watery moon;
And the imperial votaress passèd on,
In maiden meditation, fancy-free.
Yet mark'd I where the bolt of Cupid fell:
It fell upon a little western flower,—
Before milk-white, now purple with love's wound,—
And maidens call it love-in-idleness.

From THE MERCHANT OF VENICE

Lorenzo
The moon shines bright!—In such a night as this,
When the sweet wind did gently kiss the trees,
And they did make no noise; in such a night,
Troilus, methinks, mounted the Trojan walls,
And sigh'd his soul toward the Grecian tents,
Where Cressid lay that night.

*

In such a night
Stood Dido with a willow in her hand
Upon the wild sea-banks, and wav'd her love
To come again to Carthage.

*

How sweet the moonlight sleeps upon this bank!
Here will we sit, and let the sounds of music
Creep in our ears; soft stillness and the night
Become the touches of sweet harmony.
Sit, Jessica. Look how the floor of heaven
Is thick inlaid with patines of bright gold;
There's not the smallest orb which thou behold'st
But in his motion like an angel sings,
Still quiring to the young ey'd cherubims:
Such harmony is in immortal souls:
But, whilst this muddy vesture of decay
Doth grossly close it in, we cannot hear it.—
Come, ho, and wake Diana with a hymn;
With sweetest touches pierce your mistress' ear,
And draw her home with music.

From KING HENRY V

Chorus
O for a Muse of fire, that would ascend
The brightest heaven of invention!
A kingdom for a stage, princes to act,
And monarchs to behold the swelling scene!
Then should the warlike Harry, like himself,
Assume the port of Mars; and at his heels,
Leash'd in like hounds, should famine, sword, and
    fire,
Crouch for employment. But pardon, gentles all,
The flat unraisèd spirit that hath dar'd
On this unworthy scaffold to bring forth
So great an object; can this cockpit hold
The vasty fields of France? or may we cram
Within this wooden O the very casques

That did affright the air at Agincourt?
O, pardon! since a crooked figure may
Attest in little place a million;
And let us, ciphers to this great accompt,
On your imaginary forces work.
Suppose within the girdle of these walls
Are now confin'd two mighty monarchies,
Whose high uprearèd and abutting fronts
The perilous narrow ocean parts asunder:
Piece out our imperfections with your thoughts:
Into a thousand parts divide one man,
And make imaginary puissance;
Think, when we talk of horses, that you see them
Printing their proud hoofs i' the receiving earth;
For 'tis your thoughts that now must deck our kings,
Carry them here and there; jumping o'er times,
Turning the accomplishment of many years
Into an hour-glass: for the which supply,
Admit me Chorus to this history;
Who, prologue-like, your humble patience pray,
Gently to hear, kindly to judge, our play.

From KING RICHARD III

King Richard
My conscience hath a thousand several tongues,
And every tongue brings in a several tale,
And every tale condemns me for a villain.
Perjury, perjury, in the high'st degree;
Murder, stern murder, in the dir'st degree;
All several sins, all us'd in each degree,
Throng to the bar, crying all, Guilty! guilty!
I shall despair. There is no creature loves me;

4—B.H.

And if I die no soul shall pity me:
Nay, wherefore should they,—since that I myself
Find in myself no pity to myself?

From JULIUS CAESAR

Antony
O, pardon me, thou bleeding piece of earth,
That I am meek and gentle with these butchers!
Thou art the ruins of the noblest man
That ever livèd in the tide of times.
Woe to the hand that shed this costly blood!
Over thy wounds now do I prophesy,—
Which like dumb mouths do ope their ruby lips,
To beg the voice and utterance of my tongue,—
A curse shall light upon the limbs of men;
Domestic fury and fierce civil strife
Shall cumber all the parts of Italy;
Blood and destruction shall be so in use,
And dreadful objects so familiar,
That mothers shall but smile when they behold
Their infants quarter'd with the hands of war;
All pity chok'd with custom of fell deeds:
And Caesar's spirit, ranging for revenge,
With Ate by his side come hot from hell,
Shall in these confines with a monarch's voice
Cry *Havoc*, and let slip the dogs of war.

*

If you have tears, prepare to shed them now.
You all do know this mantle: I remember
The first time ever Caesar put it on;
'Twas on a summer's evening, in his tent,
That day he overcame the Nervii:—

Look! in this place ran Cassius' dagger through:
See what a rent the envious Casca made:
Through this the well-belovèd Brutus stabb'd;
And, as he pluck'd his cursèd steel away,
Mark how the blood of Caesar follow'd it,
As rushing out of doors, to be resolv'd
If Brutus so unkindly knock'd or no;
For Brutus, as you know, was Caesar's angel:
Judge, O you gods, how dearly Caesar loved him!
This was the most unkindest cut of all;
For when the noble Caesar saw him stab,
Ingratitude, more strong than traitor's arms,
Quite vanquish'd him: then burst his mighty heart;
And, in his mantle muffling up his face,
Even at the base of Pompey's statue,
Which all the while ran blood, great Caesar fell.
O, what a fall was there, my countrymen!
Then I, and you, and all of us fell down,
Whilst bloody treason flourish'd over us.
O, now you weep; and I perceive you feel
The dint of pity: these are gracious drops.
Kind souls, what, weep you when you but behold
Our Caesar's vesture wounded? Look you here,
Here is himself, marr'd, as you see, with traitors.

From KING LEAR

Lear to Cordelia
Pray, do not mock me:
I am a very foolish fond old man,
Fourscore and upward, not an hour more nor less;
And, to deal plainly,
I fear I am not in my perfect mind.
Methinks I should know you, and know this man;

Yet I am doubtful: for I am mainly ignorant
What place this is; and all the skill I have
Remembers not these garments; nor I know not
Where I did lodge last night. Do not laugh at me;
For, as I am a man, I think this lady
To be my child Cordelia.

*

No, no, no, no! Come, let's away to prison:
We two alone will sing like birds i' the cage:
When thou dost ask me blessing I'll kneel down
And ask of thee forgiveness: so we'll live,
And pray, and sing, and tell old tales, and laugh
At gilded butterflies, and hear poor rogues
Talk of court news; and we'll talk with them too,—
Who loses and who wins; who's in, who's out;—
And take upon's the mystery of things
As if we were God's spies: and we'll wear out
In a wall'd prison packs and sects of great ones
That ebb and flow by the moon.

From ROMEO AND JULIET

Juliet
Come, night;—come, Romeo,—come, thou day in
    night;
For thou wilt lie upon the wings of night
Whiter than new snow on a raven's back.—
Come, gentle night,—come, loving black-brow'd
    night,
Give me my Romeo; and, when he shall die,
Take him and cut him out in little stars,
And he will make the face of heaven so fine
That all the world will be in love with night,
And pay no worship to the garish sun.

*

Romeo
How oft when men are at the point of death
Have they been merry! which their keepers call
A lightning before death: O, how may I
Call this a lightning?—O my love! my wife!
Death, that hath suck'd the honey of thy breath,
Hath had no power yet upon thy beauty:
Thou art not conquer'd; beauty's ensign yet
Is crimson in thy lips and in thy cheeks,
And death's pale flag is not advancèd there.

From MACBETH

Macbeth
Methought I heard a voice cry, *Sleep no more!*
Macbeth does murder sleep,—the innocent sleep,
Sleep that knits up the ravell'd sleeve of care,
The death of each day's life, sore labour's bath,
Balm of hurt minds, great nature's second course,
Chief nourisher in life's feast.

*

She should have died hereafter;
There would have been a time for such a word.—
To-morrow, and to-morrow, and to-morrow,
Creeps in this petty pace from day to day,
To the last syllable of recorded time;
And all our yesterdays have lighted fools
The way to dusty death. Out, out, brief candle!
Life's but a walking shadow; a poor player,
That struts and frets his hour upon the stage,
And then is heard no more: it is a tale
Told by an idiot, full of sound and fury,
Signifying nothing.

From HAMLET

Hamlet
O, what a rogue and peasant slave am I!
Is it not monstrous that this player here,
But in a fiction, in a dream of passion,
Could force his soul so to his own conceit
That from her working all his visage wan'd;
Tears in his eyes, distraction in's aspect,
A broken voice, and his whole function suiting
With forms to his conceit? And all for nothing!
For Hecuba?
What's Hecuba to him or he to Hecuba,
That he should weep for her? What would he do,
Had he the motive and the cue for passion
That I have? He would drown the stage with tears,
And cleave the general ear with horrid speech;
Make mad the guilty, and appal the free;
Confound the ignorant, and amaze, indeed,
The very faculties of eyes and ears.

*

To be, or not to be,—that is the question:—
Whether 'tis nobler in the mind to suffer
The slings and arrows of outrageous fortune,
Or to take arms against a sea of troubles,
And by opposing end them?—To die,—to sleep,—
No more; and by a sleep to say we end
The heart-ache and the thousand natural shocks
That flesh is heir to,—'tis a consummation
Devoutly to be wish'd. To die,—to sleep;—
To sleep! perchance to dream:—ay, there's the rub;
For in that sleep of death what dreams may come,
When we have shuffled off this mortal coil,

Must give us pause; there's the respect
That makes calamity of so long life;
For who would bear the whips and scorns of time,
The oppressor's wrong, the proud man's contumely,
The pangs of despis'd love, the law's delay,
The insolence of office, and the spurns
That patient merit of the unworthy takes,
When he himself might his quietus make
With a bare bodkin? who would fardels bear,
To grunt and sweat under a weary life,
But that the dread of something after death,—
The undiscover'd country, from whose bourn
No traveller returns,—puzzles the will,
And makes us rather bear those ills we have
Than fly to others that we know not of?
Thus conscience does make cowards of us all;
And thus the native hue of resolution
Is sicklied o'er with the pale cast of thought;
And enterprises of great pith and moment,
With this regard, their currents turn awry,
And lose the name of action.

From OTHELLO

Iago
Not poppy, nor mandragora,
Nor all the drowsy syrups of the world,
Shall ever medicine thee to that sweet sleep
Which thou ow'dst yesterday.

*

Othello
It is the cause, it is the cause, my soul,—
Let me not name it to you, you chaste stars!—

It is the cause.—Yet I'll not shed her blood;
Nor scar that whiter skin of hers than snow,
And smooth as monumental alabaster.
Yet she must die, else she'll betray more men.
Put out the light, and then put out the light:
If I quench thee, thou flaming minister,
I can again thy former light restore,
Should I repent me:—but once put out thy light,
Thou cunning'st pattern of excelling nature,
I know not where is that Promethean heat
That can thy light relume.

From ANTONY AND CLEOPATRA

Cleopatra
Give me to drink mandragora,
That I might sleep out this great gap of time
My Antony is away.

*

O Charmian,
Where think'st thou he is now? Stands he or sits he?
Or does he walk? or is he on his horse?
O happy horse to bear the weight of Antony!
Do bravely, horse! for wott'st thou whom thou
     mov'st?
The demi-Atlas of this earth, the arm
And burgonet of men.—He's speaking now,
Or murmuring, *Where's my serpent of old Nile?*
For so he calls me.

*

Enobarbus
The barge she sat in, like a burnish'd throne,
Burn'd on the water: the poop was beaten gold;
Purple the sails, and so perfumèd that

The winds were love-sick with them; the oars were
   silver,
Which to the tune of flutes kept stroke, and made
The water which they beat to follow faster,
As amorous of their strokes. For her own person,
It beggar'd all description: she did lie
In her pavilion, cloth-of-gold, of tissue,
O'er-picturing that Venus where we see
The fancy out-work nature: on each side her
Stood pretty dimpled boys, like smiling Cupids,
With divers-colour'd fans, whose wind did seem
To glow the delicate cheeks which they did cool,
And what they undid did.

*

Her gentlewomen, like the Nereids,
So many mermaids, tended her i' the eyes,
And made their bends adornings: at the helm
A seeming mermaid steers: the silken tackle
Swell with the touches of those flower-soft hands
That yarely frame the office. From the barge
A strange invisible perfume hits the sense
Of the adjacent wharfs. The city cast
Her people out upon her; and Antony,
Enthron'd i' the market-place, did sit alone,
Whistling to the air; which, but for vacancy,
Had gone to gaze on Cleopatra too,
And made a gap in nature.

*

Age cannot wither her, nor custom stale
Her infinite variety: other women cloy
The appetites they feed; but she makes hungry
Where most she satisfies.

*

Cleopatra
Antony's dead!—
If thou say so, villain, thou kill'st thy mistress:
But well and free,
If thou so yield him, there is gold, and here
My bluest veins to kiss,—a hand that kings
Have lipp'd, and trembled kissing.

*

Antony
Unarm, Eros; the long day's task is done,
And we must sleep.

*

I will o'ertake thee, Cleopatra, and
Weep for my pardon. So it must be, for now
All length is torture.—Since the torch is out,
Lie down, and stray no further: now all labour
Mars what it does; yea, very force entangles
Itself with strength: seal then, and all is done.—
Eros!—I come, my queen.—Eros!—stay for me:
Where souls do couch on flowers, we'll hand in
    hand,
And with our sprightly port make the ghosts gaze:
Dido and her Aeneas shall want troops,
And all the haunt be ours.

*

I am dying, Egypt, dying; only
I here importune death awhile, until
Of many thousand kisses the poor last
I lay upon thy lips.

*

Cleopatra
The crown o' the earth doth melt.—My lord!—
O, wither'd is the garland of the war,
The soldier's pole is fallen: young boys and girls
Are level now with men: the odds is gone,
And there is nothing left remarkable
Beneath the visiting moon.

*

All's but naught:
Patience is sottish, and impatience does
Become a dog that's mad: then is it sin
To rush into the secret house of death
Ere death dare come to us?

*

Where art thou, death?
Come hither, come! come, come, and take a queen
Worth many babes and beggars!

*

I dream'd there was an emperor Antony:—
O, such another sleep, that I might see
But such another man!

*

His face was as the heavens; and therein stuck
A sun and moon, which kept their course, and
    lighted
The little O, the earth.

*

His legs bestrid the ocean: his rear'd arm
Crested the world: his voice was propertied
As all the tunèd spheres, and that to friends;
But when he meant to quail and shake the orb,
He was as rattling thunder. For his bounty,
There was no winter in't; an autumn 'twas

That grew the more by reaping: his delights
Were dolphin-like; they show'd his back above
The element they liv'd in: in his livery
Walk'd crowns and crownets; realms and islands
   were
As plates dropp'd from his pocket.

*

Give me my robe, put on my crown; I have
Immortal longings in me: now no more
The juice of Egypt's grape shall moist this lip.
Yare, yare, good Iras; quick.—Methinks I hear
Antony call; I see him rouse himself
To praise my noble act; I hear him mock
The luck of Cæsar, which the gods give men
To excuse their after wrath. Husband, I come:
Now to that name my courage prove my title!
I am fire and air; my other elements
I give to baser life. So, have you done?
Come then, and take the last warmth of my lips.
Farewell, kind Charmian;—Iras, long farewell.

*

Iras
Finish, good lady; the bright day is done,
And we are for the dark.

*

Charmian
Now boast thee, death, in thy possession lies
A lass unparallel'd.—Downy windows, close;
And golden Phoebus never be beheld
Of eyes again so royal! Your crown's awry;
I'll mend it and then play.

THE 17TH CENTURY: "FAIR AND FLAGRANT THINGS"

TEARS

Weep you no more, sad fountains;
What need you flow so fast?
Look how the snowy mountains
Heaven's sun doth gently waste!
But my Sun's heavenly eyes
View not your weeping,
That now lies sleeping
Softly, now softly lies
Sleeping.

Sleep is a reconciling,
A rest that peace begets;
Doth not the sun rise smiling
When fair at even he sets?
Rest you then, rest, sad eyes!
Melt not in weeping,
While she lies sleeping
Softly, now softly lies
Sleeping.

Anonymous

MY LADY'S TEARS

I saw my Lady weep,
And Sorrow proud to be advancèd so
In those fair eyes where all perfections keep.
Her face was full of woe;
But such a woe (believe me) as wins more hearts
Than Mirth can do with her enticing parts.

Sorrow was there made fair,
And Passion wise; Tears a delightful thing;
Silence beyond all speech, a wisdom rare:
She made her sighs to sing,
And all things with so sweet a sadness move
As made my heart at once both grieve and love.

O fairer than aught else
The world can show, leave off in time to grieve!
Enough, enough: your joyful look excels:
Tears kill the heart, believe.
O strive not to be excellent in woe,
Which only breeds your beauty's overthrow.

Anonymous

THERE IS A LADY
SWEET AND KIND

There is a Lady sweet and kind,
Was never face so pleas'd my mind;
I did but see her passing by,
And yet I love her till I die.

Her gesture, motion, and her smiles,
Her wit, her voice my heart beguiles,
Beguiles my heart, I know not why,
And yet I love her till I die.

Cupid is wingèd and doth range;
Her country so my love doth change:
But change she earth, or change she sky,
Yet will I love her till I die.

Anonymous

HELEN OF KIRCONNELL

I wish I were where Helen lies,
Night and day on me she cries;
O that I were where Helen lies,
On fair Kirconnell lea!

Curst be the heart that thought the thought,
And curst the hand that fired the shot,
When in my arms burd Helen dropt,
And died to succour me!

O think na ye my heart was sair,
When my Love dropp'd and spak nae mair!
There did she swoon wi' meikle care,
On fair Kirconnell lea.

As I went down the water side,
None but my foe to be my guide,
None but my foe to be my guide,
On fair Kirconnell lea;

I lighted down my sword to draw,
I hackèd him in pieces sma',
I hackèd him in pieces sma',
For her sake that died for me.

O Helen fair, beyond compare!
I'll mak a garland o' thy hair,
Shall bind my heart for evermair,
Until the day I die!

O that I were where Helen lies!
Night and day on me she cries;
Out of my bed she bids me rise,
Says, "Haste, and come to me!"

O Helen fair! O Helen chaste!
If I were with thee, I'd be blest,
Where thou lies low and taks thy rest,
On fair Kirconnell lea.

I wish my grave were growing green,
A winding-sheet drawn owre my e'en,
And I in Helen's arms lying,
On fair Kirconnell lea.

I wish I were where Helen lies!
Night and day on me she cries;
And I am weary of the skies,
For her sake that died for me.

Anonymous

THE GOOD-MORROW

I wonder, by my troth, what thou and I
Did, till we loved? were we not wean'd till then?
But suck'd on country pleasures, childishly?
Or snorted we in the Seven Sleepers' den?
'Twas so; but this, all pleasures fancies be;
If ever any beauty I did see,
Which I desired, and got, 'twas but a dream of thee.

And now good-morrow to our waking souls,
Which watch not one another out of fear;
For love all love of other sights controls,
And makes one little room an everywhere.
Let sea-discoverers to new worlds have gone;
Let maps to other worlds on worlds have shown;
Let us possess one world; each hath one, and is one.

My face in thine eye, thine in mine appears,
And true plain hearts do in the faces rest;
Where can we find two better hemispheres
Without sharp north, without declining west?
Whatever dies, was not mix'd equally;
If our two loves be one, or thou and I
Love so alike that none can slacken, none can die.

John Donne

From THE ECSTACY

Where, like a pillow on a bed,
A pregnant bank swell'd up, to rest
The violet's reclining head,
Sat we two, one another's best.

Our hands were firmly cémented
By a fast balm, which thence did spring;
Our eye-beams twisted, and did thread
Our eyes upon one double string.

So t'entergraft our hands, as yet
Was all the means to make us one;
And pictures in our eyes to get
Was all our propagation.

As, 'twixt two equal armies, Fate
Suspends uncertain victory,
Our souls—which to advance their state,
Were gone out—hung 'twixt her and me.

And whilst our souls negotiate there,
We like sepulchral statues lay;
All day, the same our postures were,
And we said nothing, all the day.

John Donne

LOVE'S DEITY

I long to talk with some old lover's ghost,
Who died before the god of love was born.
I cannot think that he, who then loved most,
Sunk so low as to love one which did scorn.
But since this god produced a destiny,
And that vice-nature, custom, lets it be,
I must love her that loves not me.

Sure, they which made him god, meant not so much,
Nor he in his young godhead practised it.
But when an even flame two hearts did touch,
His office was indulgently to fit
Actives to passives. Correspondency
Only his subject was; it cannot be
Love, till I love her, who loves me.

But every modern god will now extend
His vast prerogative as far as Jove.
To rage, to lust, to write to, to commend,
All is the purlieu of the god of love.

O! were we waken'd by this tyranny
To ungod this child again, it could not be
I should love her, who loves not me.

Rebel and atheist too, why murmur I,
As though I felt the worst that love could do?
Love might make me leave loving, or might try
A deeper plague, to make her love me too;
Which, since she loves before, I'm loth to see.
Falsehood is worse than hate; and that must be,
If she whom I love, should love me.

John Donne

TO THE VIRGINS, TO MAKE MUCH OF TIME

Gather ye rose-buds while ye may,
Old Time is still a-flying:
And this same flower that smiles to-day,
To-morrow will be dying.

The glorious Lamp of Heaven, the Sun,
The higher he's a-getting
The sooner will his race be run,
And nearer he's to setting.

That age is best which is the first,
When youth and blood are warmer;
But being spent, the worse, and worst
Times, still succeed the former.

Then be not coy, but use your time;
And while ye may, go marry:
For having lost but once your prime,
You may for ever tarry.

Robert Herrick

DELIGHT IN DISORDER

A sweet disorder in the dress
Kindles in clothes a wantonness:
A lawn about the shoulders thrown
Into a fine distractión:
An erring lace, which here and there
Enthrals the crimson stomacher:
A cuff neglectful, and thereby
Ribbands to flow confusedly:
A winning wave, deserving note,
In the tempestuous petticoat:
A careless shoe-string, in whose tie
I see a wild civility:
Do more bewitch me than when art
Is too precise in every part.

Robert Herrick

DISCIPLINE

Throw away thy rod,
Throw away thy wrath;
O my God,
Take the gentle path.

For my heart's desire
Unto thine is bent;
I aspire
To a full consent.

Not a word or look
I affect to own,
But by book,
And thy Book alone.

Though I fail, I weep;
Though I halt in pace,
Yet I creep
To the throne of grace.

Then let wrath remove,
Love will do the deed;
For with love
Stony hearts will bleed.

Love is swift of foot;
Love's a man of war,
And can shoot,
And can hit from far.

Who can 'scape his bow?
That which wrought on thee,
Brought thee low,
Needs must work on me.

Throw away thy rod:
Though man frailties hath,
Thou art God;
Throw away thy wrath.

George Herbert

THE PULLEY

When God at first made man,
Having a glass of blessings standing by—
Let us (said he) pour on him all we can;
Let the world's riches, which dispersèd lie,
Contract into a span.

So strength first made a way,
Then beauty flow'd, then wisdom, honour, pleasure:
When almost all was out, God made a stay,
Perceiving that, alone of all his treasure,
Rest in the bottom lay.

For if I should (said he)
Bestow this jewel also on my creature,
He would adore my gifts instead of me,
And rest in nature, not the God of nature:
So both should losers be.

Yet let him keep the rest,
But keep them with repining restlessness;
Let him be rich and weary, that at least,
If goodness lead him not, yet weariness
May toss him to my breast.

George Herbert

LOVE

Love bade me welcome; yet my soul drew back,
Guilty of dust and sin.
But quick-eyed Love, observing me grow slack
From my first entrance in,
Drew nearer to me, sweetly questioning
If I lack'd anything.

"A guest," I answer'd, "worthy to be here:"
Love said, "You shall be he."
"I, the unkind, ungrateful? Ah my dear,
I cannot look on thee."
Love took my hand and smiling did reply,
"Who made the eyes but I?"

"Truth, Lord; but I have marr'd them: let my shame
Go where it doth deserve."
"And know you not," says Love, "Who bore the
  blame?"
"My dear, then I will serve."
"You must sit down," says Love, "and taste my
  meat."
So I did sit and eat.

George Herbert

THE COLLAR
(probably the old spelling of choler)

I struck the board, and cried, "No more;
I will abroad.
What, shall I ever sigh and pine?
My lines and life are free; free as the road,
Loose as the wind, as large as store.
Shall I be still in suit?
Have I no harvest but a thorn
To let me blood, and not restore
What I have lost with cordial fruit?
Sure there was wine
Before my sighs did dry it; there was corn
Before my tears did drown it;
Is the year only lost to me?
Have I no bays to crown it,
No flowers, no garlands gay? all blasted,
All wasted?
Not so, my heart; but there is fruit,
And thou hast hands.
Recover all thy sigh-blown age
On double pleasures; leave thy cold dispute
Of what is fit and not; forsake thy cage,
Thy rope of sands,

Which petty thoughts have made; and made to thee
Good cable, to enforce and draw,
And be thy law,
While thou didst wink and wouldst not see.
Away! take heed;
I will abroad.
Call in thy death's-head there, tie up thy fears;
He that forbears
To suit and serve his need
Deserves his load."
But as I raved and grew more fierce and wild
At every word,
Methought I heard one calling, "Child";
And I replied, "My Lord."

George Herbert

DEATH THE LEVELLER

The glories of our blood and state
Are shadows, not substantial things;
There is no armour against fate;
Death lays his icy hand on kings:
Sceptre and Crown
Must tumble down,
And in the dust be equal made
With the poor crooked scythe and spade.

Some men with swords may reap the field,
And plant fresh laurels where they kill:
But their strong nerves at last must yield;
They tame but one another still:
Early or late
They stoop to fate,
And must give up their murmuring breath
When they, pale captives, creep to death.

The garlands wither on your brow;
Then boast no more your mighty deeds;
Upon Death's purple altar now
See where the victor-victim bleeds:
Your heads must come
To the cold tomb;
Only the actions of the just
Smell sweet, and blossom in their dust.

James Shirley

GO, LOVELY ROSE

Go, lovely rose—
Tell her that wastes her time and me,
That now she knows,
When I resemble her to thee,
How sweet and fair she seems to be.

Tell her that's young,
And shuns to have her graces spied,
That hadst thou sprung
In deserts where no men abide,
Thou must have uncommended died.

Small is the worth
Of beauty from the light retired:
Bid her come forth,
Suffer herself to be desired,
And not blush so to be admired.

Then die—that she
The common fate of all things rare
May read in thee;
How small a part of time they share
That are so wondrous sweet and fair!

Edmund Waller

ON HIS BLINDNESS

When I consider how my light is spent
Ere half my days, in this dark world and wide,
And that one talent which is death to hide
Lodged with me useless, though my soul more bent
To serve therewith my Maker, and present
My true account, lest he, returning, chide;
"Doth God exact day-labour, light denied?"
I fondly ask: but Patience, to prevent
That murmur, soon replies, "God doth not need
Either man's work, or his own gifts; who best
Bear his mild yoke, they serve him best; his state
Is kingly: thousands at his bidding speed,
And post o'er land and ocean without rest;
They also serve who only stand and wait."

John Milton

From LYCIDAS: *elegy on a friend drowned*

Yet once more, O ye laurels, and once more
Ye myrtles brown, with ivy never sere,
I come to pluck your berries harsh and crude,
And with forced fingers rude
Shatter your leaves before the mellowing year.
Bitter constraint, and sad occasion dear
Compels me to disturb your season due:

For Lycidas is dead, dead ere his prime,
Young Lycidas, and hath not left his peer:
Who would not sing for Lycidas? he knew
Himself to sing, and build the lofty rhyme.
He must not float upon his watery bier
Unwept, and welter to the parching wind,
Without the meed of some melodious tear.

For we were nursed upon the self-same hill,
Fed the same flock by fountain, shade, and rill.
Together both, ere the high lawns appear'd
Under the opening eye-lids of the morn,
We drove a-field, and both together heard
What time the gray-fly winds her sultry horn,
Battening our flocks with the fresh dews of night,
Oft till the star, that rose at evening bright,
Toward heaven's descent had sloped his westering
   wheel.
Meanwhile the rural ditties were not mute,
Temper'd to the oaten flute;
Rough Satyrs danced, and Fauns with cloven heel
From the glad sound would not be absent long;
And old Damaetas loved to hear our song.

Alas! what boots it with uncessant care
To tend the homely, slighted, shepherd's trade
And strictly meditate the thankless Muse?
Were it not better done, as others use,
To sport with Amaryllis in the shade,
Or with the tangles of Neaera's hair?
Fame is the spur that the clear spirit doth raise
(That last infirmity of noble mind)
To scorn delights, and live laborious days;

But the fair guerdon when we hope to find,
And think to burst out into sudden blaze,
Comes the blind Fury with the abhorrèd shears
And slits the thin-spun life. "But not the praise",
Phoebus replied, and touch'd my trembling ears;
"Fame is no plant that grows on mortal soil,
Nor in the glistering foil
Set off to the world, nor in broad rumour lies:
But lives and spreads aloft by those pure eyes
And perfect witness of all-judging Jove;
As he pronounces lastly on each deed,
Of so much fame in heaven expect thy meed."

Look homeward Angel, now, and melt with ruth:
And, O ye dolphins, waft the hapless youth.

Weep no more, woeful shepherds, weep no more,
For Lycidas, your sorrow, is not dead,
Sunk though he be beneath the watery floor;
So sinks the day-star in the ocean-bed,
And yet anon repairs his drooping head,
And tricks his beams, and with new-spangled ore,
Flames in the forehead of the morning sky:
So Lycidas sunk low, but mounted high
Through the dear might of Him that walk'd the
      waves;
Where, other groves and other streams along,
With nectar pure his oozy locks he laves,
And hears the unexpressive nuptial song,
In the blest kingdoms meek of joy and love.
There entertain him all the saints above
In solemn troops, and sweet societies,
That sing, and singing in their glory move,

And wipe the tears for ever from his eyes.
Now, Lycidas, the shepherds weep no more;
Henceforth thou art the Genius of the shore,
In thy large recompense, and shalt be good
To all that wander in that perilous flood.

Thus sang the uncouth swain to the oaks and rills,
While the still morn went out with sandals grey;
He touch'd the tender stops of various quills,
With eager thought warbling his Doric lay:
And now the sun had stretch'd out all the hills,
And now was dropt into the western bay:
At last he rose, and twitch'd his mantle blue:
To-morrow to fresh woods, and pastures new.

John Milton

WHY SO PALE AND WAN?

Why so pale and wan, fond lover?
Prithee, why so pale?
Will, when looking well can't move her,
Looking ill prevail?
Prithee, why so pale?

Why so dull and mute, young sinner?
Prithee, why so mute?
Will, when speaking well can't win her,
Saying nothing do't?
Prithee, why so mute?

Quit, quit for shame! This will not move,
This cannot take her.
If of herself she will not love,
Nothing can make her:
The devil take her!

Sir John Suckling

From WISHES TO HIS SUPPOSED
MISTRESS

Whoe'er she be—
That not impossible She
That shall command my heart and me:

I wish her Beauty,
That owes not all its duty
To gaudy tire, or glist'ring shoe-tie:

Something more than
Taffata or tissue can,
Or rampant feather, or rich fan.

A Face, that's best
By its own beauty drest,
And can alone commend the rest.

Whose native ray
Can tame the wanton day
Of gems that in their bright shades play.

Each ruby there,
Or pearl that dare appear,
Be its own blush, be its own tear.

A well-tamed Heart,
For whose more noble smart
Love may be long choosing a dart.

Eyes, that bestow
Full quivers on love's bow,
Yet pay less arrows than they owe.

Smiles, that can warm
The blood, yet teach a charm,
That chastity shall take no harm.

Blushes, that bin
The burnish of no sin,
Nor flames of aught too hot within.

Richard Crashaw

LOVE

I'll sing of Heroes, and of Kings;
In mighty numbers, mighty things,
Begin, my Muse; but lo, the strings
To my great song rebellious prove;
The strings will sound of nought but Love.
I broke them all, and put on new;
'Tis this or nothing sure will do.
These sure (said I) will me obey;
These, sure, heroic notes will play.
Straight I began with thund'ring Jove,
And all th' immortal Powers, but Love.
Love smil'd, and from my enfeebled lyre
Came gentle airs, such as inspire
Melting love, and soft desire.
Farewell then Heroes, farewell Kings,
And mighty numbers, mighty things;
Love tunes my heart just to my strings.

Abraham Cowley

6—B.H.

TO ALTHEA, FROM PRISON

When Love with unconfinèd wings
Hovers within my gates,
And my divine Althea brings
To whisper at the grates;
When I lie tangled in her hair
And fetter'd to her eye,
The gods that wanton in the air
Know no such liberty.

When flowing cups run swiftly round
With no allaying Thames,
Our careless heads with roses crown'd,
Our hearts with loyal flames;
When thirsty grief in wine we steep,
When healths and draughts go free—
Fishes that tipple in the deep
Know no such liberty.

Stone walls do not a prison make,
Nor iron bars a cage;
Minds innocent and quiet take
That for an hermitage:
If I have freedom in my love
And in my soul am free,
Angels alone, that soar above,
Enjoy such liberty.

                              Richard Lovelace

THE PROUD EGYPTIAN QUEEN

"And she washed his feet with her tears, and
wiped them with the hairs of her head."

The proud Egyptian Queen, her Roman guest,
(T'express her love in height of state, and pleasure)
With Pearl dissolv'd in Gold, did feast—
Both Food, and Treasure.

And now (dear Lord!) thy Lover, on the fair
And silver tables of thy feet, behold,
Pearl in her tears, and in her hair
Offers thee gold.

Edward Sherburne

THE GARDEN

How vainly men themselves amaze
To win the palm, the oak, or bays;
And their incessant labours see
Crowned from some single herb, or tree,
Whose short and narrow-vergèd shade
Does prudently their toils upbraid;
While all flow'rs and all trees do close
To weave the garlands of repose.

Fair Quiet, have I found thee here,
And Innocence, thy sister dear?
Mistaken long, I sought you then
In busy companies of men.
Your sacred plants, if here below,
Only among the plants will grow;
Society is all but rude
To this delicious solitude.

No white nor red was ever seen
So amorous as this lovely green.
Fond lovers, cruel as their flame,
Cut in these trees their mistress' name:
Little, alas! they know or heed
How far these beauties hers exceed!
Fair trees! wheres'e'er your barks I wound
No name shall but your own be found.

When we have run our passion's heat,
Love hither makes his best retreat.
The Gods, that mortal beauty chase,
Still in a tree did end their race;
Apollo hunted Daphne so,
Only that she might laurel grow;
And Pan did after Syrinx speed,
Not as a nymph, but for a reed.

What wondrous life is this I lead!
Ripe apples drop about my head;
The luscious clusters of the vine
Upon my mouth do crush their wine;
The nectaren, and curious peach,
Into my hands themselves do reach;
Stumbling on melons, as I pass,
Insnared with flowers, I fall on grass.

Meanwhile, the mind, from pleasure less,
Withdraws into its happiness:
The mind, that ocean where each kind
Does straight its own resemblance find;
Yet it creates, transcending these,
Far other worlds, and other seas;

Annihilating all that's made
To a green thought in a green shade.

Here at the fountain's sliding foot,
Or at some fruit-tree's mossy root,
Casting the body's vest aside,
My soul into the boughs does glide:
There like a bird it sits, and sings,
Then whets and claps its silver wings;
And, till prepared for longer flight,
Waves in its plumes the various light.

Such was that happy garden-state,
While man there walked without a mate:
After a place so pure and sweet,
What other help could yet be meet!
But 'twas beyond a mortal's share
To wander solitary there:
Two paradises 'twere in one,
To live in paradise alone!

How well the skilful gardener drew
Of flowers, and herbs, this dial new;
Where, from above, the milder sun
Does through a fragrant zodiac run;
And, as it works, the industrious bee
Computes its time as well as we.
How could such sweet and wholesome hours
Be reckon'd but with herbs and flowers!

Andrew Marvell

THE PICTURE OF LITTLE T.C. IN A PROSPECT OF FLOWERS

See with what simplicity
This nymph begins her golden days!
In the green grass she loves to lie,
And there with her fair aspect tames
The wilder flowers, and gives them names;
But only with the roses plays,
And them does tell
What colours best become them, and what smell.

Who can foretell for what high cause
This darling of the gods was born?
Yet this is she whose chaster laws
The wanton Love shall one day fear,
And, under her command severe,
See his bow broke, and ensigns torn.
Happy who can
Appease this virtuous enemy of man!

O then let me in time compound
And parley with those conquering eyes,
Ere they have tried their force to wound,
Ere with their glancing wheels they drive
In triumph over hearts that strive,
And them that yield but more despise:
Let me be laid
Where I may see the glories from some shade.

Meantime, whilst every verdant thing
Itself does at thy beauty charm,
Reform the errors of the Spring;
Make that the tulips may have share

Of sweetness, seeing they are fair,
And roses of their thorns disarm;
But most procure
That violets may a longer age endure.

But O young beauty of the woods,
Whom Nature courts with fruits and flowers,
Gather the flowers, but spare the buds;
Lest Flora, angry at thy crime
To kill her infants in their prime,
Should quickly make the example yours;
And, ere we see,
Nip, in the blossom, all our hopes and thee.

                                          Andrew Marvell

THE MOWER TO THE GLOW-WORMS

Ye living lamps, by whose dear light
The nightingale does sit so late,
And studying all the summer night,
Her matchless songs does mediate;

Ye country comets, that portend
No war, nor prince's funeral,
Shining unto no higher end
Than to presage the grass's fall;

Ye glow-worms, whose officious flame
To wandering mowers shows the way
That in the night have lost their aim,
And after foolish fires do stray;

Your courteous lights in vain you waste,
Since Juliana here is come,
For she my mind hath so displaced
That I shall never find my home.

Andrew Marvell

THE FAIR SINGER

To make a final conquest of all me,
Love did compose so sweet an enemy,
In whom both beauties to my death agree,
Joining themselves in fatal harmony;
That, while she with her eyes my heart does bind,
She with her voice might captivate my mind.

I could have fled from one but singly fair:
My disentangled soul itself might save,
Breaking the curlèd trammels of her hair.
But how should I avoid to be her slave,
Whose subtle art invisibly can wreathe
My fetters of the very air I breathe?

It had been easy fighting in some plain,
Where victory might hang in equal choice,
But all resistance against her is vain,
Who has the advantage both of eyes and voice;
And all my forces needs must be undone,
She having gainèd both the wind and sun.

Andrew Marvell

ANGUISH

My God and King! to thee
I bow my knee;
I bow my troubled soul, and greet
With my foul heart thy holy feet.
Cast it, or tread it! it shall do
Even what thou wilt, and praise thee too.

My God, could I weep blood,
Gladly I would,
Or if thou wilt give me that art,
Which through the eyes pours out the heart,
I will exhaust it all, and make
Myself all tears, a weeping lake.

O! 'tis an easy thing
To write and sing;
But to write true, unfeignèd verse
Is very hard! O God, disperse
These weights, and give my spirit leave
To act as well as to conceive!

O my God, hear my cry;
Or let me die! . . .

Henry Vaughan

THE DAWNING

Ah! what time wilt thou come? when shall that cry
"*The Bridegroom's coming!*" fill the sky?
Shall it in the evening run
When our words and works are done?
Or will thy all-surprising light
Break at midnight,

When either sleep, or some dark pleasure
Possesseth mad man without measure?
Or shall these early, fragrant hours
Unlock thy bowers
And with their blush of light descry
Thy locks crowned with eternity?

Indeed, it is the only time
That with thy glory doth best chime;
All now are stirring, ev'ry field
Full hymns doth yield,
The whole Creation shakes off night,
And for thy shadow looks the light.
Stars now vanish without number,
Sleepy planets set and slumber,
The pursy clouds disband and scatter,
All expect some sudden matter;
Not one beam triumphs, but from far
That morning-star.
Oh at what time soever thou,
Unknown to us, the heavens wilt bow,
And with thy angels in the van
Descend to judge poor careless man,
Grant I may not like puddle lie
In a corrupt security,
Where, if a traveller water crave,
He finds it dead, and in a grave.
But as this restless, vocal spring
All day and night doth run, and sing,
And though here born, yet is acquainted
Elsewhere, and flowing keeps untainted;
So let me all my busy age
In thy free services engage;

And though (while here) of force I must
Have commerce sometimes with poor dust,
And in my flesh, though vile and low,
As this doth in her channel, flow,
Yet let my course, my aim, my love
And chief acquaintance be above;
So when that day and hour shall come,
In which thyself will be the sun,
Thou'lt find me dress'd and on my way,
Watching the break of thy great day.

Henry Vaughan

THE REVIVAL

Unfold, unfold! take in his light,
Who makes thy cares more short than night.
The joys which with his day-star rise
He deals to all but drowsy eyes;
And (what the men of this world miss)
Some drops and dews of future bliss.

Hark, how the winds have chang'd their note,
And with warm whispers call thee out.
The frosts are past, the storms are gone,
And backward life at last comes on.
The lofty groves in express joys
Reply unto the turtle's voice;
And here in dust and dirt, O here
The lilies of his love appear!

Henry Vaughan

THE ECLIPSE

Whither, O whither didst thou fly
When I did grieve thine holy eye,
When thou didst mourn to see me lost,
And all thy care and counsels crost.
O do not grieve, where'er thou art!
Thy grief is an undoing smart,
Which doth not only pain, but break
My heart, and makes me blush to speak.
Thy anger I could kiss, and will:
But O thy grief, thy grief doth kill!

Henry Vaughan

THE WORLD

I saw Eternity the other night,
Like a great ring of pure and endless light,
All calm, as it was bright;
And round beneath it, Time in hours, days, years,
Driven by the spheres
Like a vast shadow moved; in which the world
And all her train were hurled.
The doting lover in his quaintest strain
Did there complain;
Near him, his lute, his fancy, and his flights,
Wit's sour delights,
With gloves, and knots, the silly snares of pleasure,
Yet his dear treasure,
All scattered lay, while he his eyes did pour
Upon a flower.

The darksome statesman, hung with weights and
  woe
Like a thick midnight-fog, moved there so slow,
He did not stay, nor go;
Condemning thoughts—like sad eclipses—scowl
Upon his soul,
And clouds of crying witnesses without
Pursu'd him with one shout.
Yet digg'd the mole, and lest his ways be found,
Worked under ground,
Where he did clutch his prey; (But one did see
That policy);
Churches and altars fed him; perjuries
Were gnats and flies;
It rained about him blood and tears; but he
Drank them as free.

The fearful miser on a heap of rust
Sate pining all his life there, did scarce trust
His own hands with the dust,
Yet would not place one piece above, but lives
In fear of thieves.
Thousands there were as frantic as himself
And hugged each one his pelf.
The downright epicure placed heaven in sense
And scorn'd pretence,
While others, slipp'd into a wide excess,
Said little less;
The weaker sort, slight trivial wares enslave,
Who think them brave;
And poor, despisèd Truth sate counting by
Their victory.

Yet some, who all this while did weep and sing,
And sing, and weep, soared up into the Ring;
But most would use no wing.
O fools (said I) thus to prefer dark night
Before true light!
To live in grots and caves, and hate the day
Because it shows the way,
The way, which from this dead and dark abode
Leads up to God,
A way where you might tread the sun, and be
More bright than he.
But as I did their madness so discuss,
One whisper'd thus,
This Ring the Bridegroom did for none provide,
But for his bride.

                                    Henry Vaughan

THE SHOWER

'Twas so, I saw thy birth. That drowsy lake
From her faint bosom breathed thee, the disease
Of her sick waters and infectious ease.
But now at even,
Too gross for heaven,
Thou fall'st in tears, and weep'st for thy mistake.

Ah! it is so with me: oft have I pressed
Heaven with a lazy breath; but fruitless this
Pierced not; love only can with quick access
Unlock the way,
When all else stray
The smoke and exhalations of the breast.

Yet, if as thou dost melt, and with thy train
Of drops make soft the Earth, my eyes could weep
O'er my hard heart, that's bound up and asleep,
Perhaps at last,
Some such showers past,
My God would give a sunshine after rain.

Henry Vaughan

SUN-DAYS

Bright shadows of true rest! some shoots of bliss,
Heaven once a week;
The next world's gladness prepossessed in this;
A day to seek
Eternity in time; the steps by which
We climb above all ages; lamps that light
Man through his heap of dark days; and the rich
And full redemption of the whole week's flight.

The pulleys unto headlong man; Time's bower;
The narrow way;
Transplanted Paradise; God's walking hour,
The cool o' th' day!
The creature's jubilee; God's parle with dust;
Heaven here; man on those hills of myrrh, and
    flowers;
Angels descending; the returns of trust;
A gleam of glory after six-days-showers.

The Church's love-feasts; Time's prerogative
And interest
Deducted from the whole; the combs, and hive,
And home of rest;

The milky way chalked out with suns; a clue
That guides through erring hours; and in full story
A taste of heaven on earth; the pledge and cue
Of a full feast; and the out-Courts of glory.

Henry Vaughan

EASTER HYMN

Death and darkness, get you packing,
Nothing now to man is lacking;
All your triumphs now are ended,
And what ADAM marred is mended;
Graves are beds now for the weary,
Death a nap, to wake more merry;
Youth now, full of pious duty,
Seeks in thee for perfect beauty;
The weak and agèd, tired with length
Of days, from thee look for new strength;
And infants with thy pangs contest
As pleasant as if with the breast.
Then, unto Him, who thus hath thrown
Even to contempt thy kingdom down,
And by his blood did us advance
Unto his own inheritance,
To Him be glory, power, praise,
From this unto the last of days!

Henry Vaughan

O DO NOT GO

O do not go, thou know'st I'll die;
My spring and fall are in thy book;
Or, if thou goest, do not deny
To lend me, though from far, one look.

My sins long since have made thee strange,
A very stranger unto me;
No morning meetings since this change,
Nor evening walks have I with thee.

Why is my God thus slow and cold,
When I am most, most sick and sad?
Well fare those blessed days of old,
When thou didst hear the weeping lad.

O do not thou do as I did,
Do not despise a love-sick heart;
What though some clouds defiance bid,
Thy sun must shine in every part.

Though I have spoiled, O spoil not thou,
Hate not thine own dear gift and token,
Poor birds sing best, and prettiest show,
When their nest is fallen and broken.

Dear Lord, restore thy ancient peace,
Thy quickening friendship, man's bright wealth;
And if thou wilt not give me ease
From sickness, give my spirit health.

Henry Vaughan

From PILGRIM'S PROGRESS

Who would true valour see,
Let him come hither;
One here will constant be,
Come wind, come weather.
There's no discouragement
Shall make him once relent
His first avow'd intent,
To be a pilgrim.

Whoso beset him round
With dismal stories,
Do but themselves confound,
His strength the more is.
No lion can him fright,
He'll with a giant fight,
But he will have a right
To be a pilgrim.

Hobgoblin, nor foul fiend,
Can daunt his spirit;
He knows he at the end
Shall life inherit.
Then fancies fly away,
He'll fear not what men say,
He'll labour night and day
To be a pilgrim.

John Bunyan

ON CHARLES II

Here lies our sovereign Lord the King,
Whose word no man relies on,
Who never said a foolish thing
Nor ever did a wise one.

The Earl of Rochester

THE CHOICE

Grant me, indulgent Heaven! a rural seat,
Rather contemptible than great!
Where, though I taste Life's sweets, still I may be
Athirst for Immortality!
I would have business; but exempt from strife!
A private, but an active life!
A Conscience bold, and punctual to his charge!
My stock of Health or Patience large!
Some books I'd have, and some acquaintance too;
But very good, and very few!
Then (if one mortal two such grants may crave!)
From silent life, I'd steal into my grave!

Nahum Tate

THE SOLDIER'S DEATH

Trail all your pikes, dispirit every drum,
March in a slow procession from afar,
Ye silent, ye dejected men of war!
Be still the hautboys, and the flute be dumb!
Display no more, in vain, the lofty banner;
For see! where on the bier before ye lies
The pale, the fall'n, th' untimely Sacrifice
To your mistaken Shrine, to your false Idol Honour.

Anne, Countess of Winchilsea

THE 18 TH
CENTURY: SONGS
FORMALISM AND
WILLIAM BLAKE

From THE SAILOR'S CONSOLATION

One night came on a hurricane,
The sea was mountains rolling,
When Barney Buntline turned his quid
And said to Billy Bowling:
"A strong sou'-wester's blowing, Billy,
Can't you hear it roar now?
Lord help 'em, how I pities all
Unhappy folks on shore now!

"And often have we seamen heard
How men are killed or undone
By overturns in carriages,
And thieves, and fires, in London;
We've heard what risks all landsmen run,
From noblemen to tailors;
So, Billy, let's thank Providence
That you and I are sailors."

                                    Anonymous

WILL HE NO COME BACK AGAIN?

Royal Charlie's now awa,
Safely owre the friendly main;
Mony a heart will break in twa,
Should he ne'er come back again.
Will you no come back again?
Will you no come back again?
Better lo'ed you'll never be,
And will you no come back again?

Sweet the lav'rock's note and lang,
Lilting wildly up the glen;
And aye the o'erword o' the sang
Is "Will he no come back again?"
Will he no come back again, &c.

Anonymous

YOU BEAT YOUR PATE

You beat your pate, and fancy wit will come:
Knock as you please, there's nobody at home.

Alexander Pope

"KNOW THEN THYSELF . . ."

Know then thyself, presume not God to scan;
The proper study of mankind is Man.
Plac'd on this isthmus of a middle state,
A being darkly wise, and rudely great:
With too much knowledge for the sceptic side,
With too much weakness for the stoic's pride,
He hangs between; in doubt to act, or rest;
In doubt to deem himself a god, or beast;
In doubt his mind or body to prefer;
Born but to die, and reas'ning but to err;
Alike in ignorance, his reason such,
Whether he thinks too little, or too much:
Chaos of thought and passion, all confus'd;
Still by himself abus'd, or disabus'd;
Created half to rise, and half to fall;
Great lord of all things, yet a prey to all;
Sole judge of truth, in endless error hurl'd:
The glory, jest and riddle of the world!

Alexander Pope

SALLY IN OUR ALLEY

Of all the girls that are so smart
There's none like pretty Sally;
She is the darling of my heart,
And she lives in our alley.
There is no lady in the land
Is half so sweet as Sally;
She is the darling of my heart,
And she lives in our alley.

Her father he makes cabbage-nets,
And through the streets does cry 'em;
Her mother she sells laces long
To such as please to buy 'em:
But sure such folks could ne'er beget
So sweet a girl as Sally!
She is the darling of my heart,
And she lives in our alley.

When she is by, I leave my work,
I love her so sincerely;
My master comes like any Turk,
And bangs me most severely:
But let him bang his bellyful,
I'll bear it all for Sally;
She is the darling of my heart,
And she lives in our alley.

Of all the days that's in the week
I dearly love but one day—
And that's the day that comes betwixt
A Saturday and Monday;

For then I'm drest all in my best
To walk abroad with Sally;
She is the darling of my heart,
And she lives in our alley.

My master carries me to church
And often am I blamèd
Because I leave him in the lurch
As soon as text is namèd;
I leave the church in sermon-time
And slink away to Sally;
She is the darling of my heart,
And she lives in our alley.

When Christmas comes about again,
O, then I shall have money;
I'll hoard it up, and box it all,
I'll give it to my honey:
I would it were ten thousand pound,
I'd give it all to Sally;
She is the darling of my heart,
And she lives in our alley.

My master and the neighbours all,
Make game of me and Sally,
And, but for her, I'd better be
A slave and row a galley;
But when my seven long years are out,
O, then I'll marry Sally;
O, then we'll wed, and then we'll bed—
But not in our alley!

Henry Carey

From ELEGY WRITTEN IN A COUNTRY CHURCHYARD

The Curfew tolls the knell of parting day,
The lowing herd wind slowly o'er the lea,
The plowman homeward plods his weary way,
And leaves the world to darkness and to me.

Now fades the glimmering landscape on the sight,
And all the air a solemn stillness holds,
Save where the beetle wheels his droning flight,
And drowsy tinklings lull the distant folds;

Save that from yonder ivy-mantled tow'r
The moping owl does to the moon complain
Of such as, wand'ring near her secret bow'r,
Molest her ancient solitary reign.

Beneath those rugged elms, that yew-tree's shade,
Where heaves the turf in many a mould'ring heap,
Each in his narrow cell for ever laid,
The rude Forefathers of the hamlet sleep.

Let not Ambition mock their useful toil,
Their homely joys, and destiny obscure;
Nor Grandeur hear with a disdainful smile
The short and simple annals of the poor.

The boast of heraldry, the pomp of pow'r,
And all that beauty, all that wealth e'er gave,
Awaits alike th' inevitable hour:
The paths of glory lead but to the grave.

Can storied urn or animated bust
Back to its mansion call the fleeting breath?
Can Honour's voice provoke the silent dust,
Or Flatt'ry soothe the dull cold ear of death?

Perhaps in this neglected spot is laid
Some heart once pregnant with celestial fire;
Hands, that the rod of empire might have sway'd,
Or waked to ecstasy the living lyre.

Full many a gem of purest ray serene
The dark unfathom'd caves of ocean bear:
Full many a flower is born to blush unseen,
And waste its sweetness on the desert air.

Some village Hampden that with dauntless breast
The little tyrant of his fields withstood,
Some mute inglorious Milton here may rest,
Some Cromwell guiltless of his country's blood.

Far from the madding crowd's ignoble strife
Their sober wishes never learn'd to stray;
Along the cool sequester'd vale of life
They kept the noiseless tenor of their way.

Yet ev'n these bones from insult to protect
Some frail memorial still erected nigh,
With uncouth rhymes and shapeless sculpture
    deck'd,
Implores the passing tribute of a sigh.

Thomas Gray

ON THE PHRASE "TO KILL TIME"

There's scarce a point whereon mankind agree
So well, as in their boast of killing me:
I boast of nothing, but, when I've a mind,
I think I can be even with mankind.

Translated from Voltaire

THE CALL

Sound, sound the clarion, fill the fife!
Throughout the sensual world proclaim,
One crowded hour of glorious life
Is worth an age without a name.

Thomas Osbert Mordaunt

AN EPITAPH

Like thee I once have stemm'd the sea of life,
Like thee have languish'd after empty joys,
Like thee have labour'd in the stormy strife,
Been grieved for trifles, and amused with toys.

Forget my frailties; thou art also frail:
Forgive my lapses; for thyself may'st fall:
Nor read unmoved my artless tender tale—
I was a friend, O man, to thee, to all.

James Beattie

From LINES ON RECEIVING HIS MOTHER'S PICTURE

O that those lips had language! Life has passed
With me but roughly since I heard thee last.
Those lips are thine—thy own sweet smiles I see,
The same that oft in childhood solaced me;
Voice only fails, else how distinct they say,
"Grieve not, my Child—chase all thy fears away!'

My mother! when I learnt that thou wast dead,
Say, wast thou conscious of the tears I shed?
Hovered thy spirit o'er thy sorrowing son,
Wretch even then, life's journey just begun?
Perhaps thou gav'st me, though unseen, a kiss;
Perhaps a tear, if souls can weep in bliss—
Ah, that maternal smile! it answers—yes.
I heard the bell tolled on thy burial day,
I saw the hearse that bore thee slow away,
And, turning from my nursery window, drew
A long, long sigh, and wept a last adieu!
But was it such?—It was.—Where thou art gone
Adieus and farewells are a sound unknown.
May I but meet thee on that peaceful shore
The parting word shall pass my lips no more!

Where once we dwelt our name is heard no more,
Children not thine have trod my nursery floor;
And where the gardener Robin, day by day,
Drew me to school along the public way,
Delighted with my bauble coach, and wrapped
In scarlet mantle warm, and velvet-capt,
'Tis now become a history little known,
That once we called the pastoral house our own.

Could Time, his flight reversed, restore the hours,
When, playing with thy vesture's tissued flowers,
The violet, the pink, the jessamine,
I pricked them into paper with a pin
(And thou wast happier than myself the while,
Wouldst softly speak, and stroke my head and smile),
Could those few pleasant days again appear,
Might one wish bring them, would I wish them
    here?
I would not trust my heart—the dear delight
Seems so to be desired, perhaps I might—
But no—what here we call our life is such,
So little to be loved, and thou so much,
That I should ill requite thee to constrain
Thy unbound spirit into bonds again.

Yet, O the thought that thou art safe, and he!
That thought is joy, arrive what may to me.
My boast is not that I deduce my birth
From loins enthroned, and rulers of the earth;
But higher far my proud pretensions rise—
The son of parents passed into the skies.
And now, farewell—Time unrevoked has run
His wonted course, yet what I wished is done.
By contemplation's help, not sought in vain,
I seem to have lived my childhood o'er again;
To have renewed the joys that once were mine,
Without the sin of violating thine;
And, while the wings of Fancy still are free,
And I can view this mimic show of thee,
Time has but half succeeded in his theft—
Thyself removed, thy power to soothe me left.

William Cowper

From PETER GRIMES

"I am escaped," he said, when none pursued;
When none attack'd him, "I am unsubdued";
"Oh pleasing pangs of love!" he sang again,
Cold to the joy, and stranger to the pain.
E'en in his age would he address the young,
"I, too, have felt those fires, and they are strong";
But from the time he left his favourite maid,
To ancient females his devoirs were paid:
And still they miss him after morning prayer.

Habit with him was all the test of truth:
"It must be right; I've done it from my youth."

Though mild benevolence our priest possess'd,
'Twas but by wishes or by words express'd.
Circles in water, as they wider flow,
The less conspicuous in their progress grow,
And when at last they touch upon the shore,
Distinction ceases, and they're view'd no more.
His love, like that last circle, all embraced
But with effect that never could be traced.

Now rests our Vicar. They who knew him best,
Proclaim his life t'have been entirely rest . . .

George Crabbe

THE TYGER

(From the first and second drafts of this poem)

Tyger, Tyger, burning bright
In the forests of the night,
What immortal hand or eye
Dare frame thy fearful symmetry?

Burnt in distant deeps or skies
The cruel fire of thine eyes?
On what wings dare he aspire?
What the hand dare seize the fire?

And what shoulder and what art
Could twist the sinews of thy heart?
And when thy heart began to beat
What dread hand and what dread feet

Could fetch it from the furnace deep
And in thy horrid ribs dare steep?
In what clay and in what mould
Were thy eyes of fury roll'd?

Where the hammer? Where the chain?
In what furnace was thy brain?
What the anvil? What dread grasp
Dare its deadly terrors clasp?

When the stars threw down their spears
And water'd heaven with their tears
Dare he laugh his work to see?
Dare he who made the lamb make thee?

Tyger, Tyger, burning bright
In the forests of the night,
What immortal hand and eye
Dare frame thy fearful symmetry?
William Blake

THE DIVINE IMAGE

To Mercy, Pity, Peace, and Love
All pray in their distress;
And to these virtues of delight
Return their thankfulness.

For Mercy, Pity, Peace, and Love
Is God, our father dear,
And Mercy, Pity, Peace, and Love
Is Man, his child and care.

For Mercy has a human heart,
Pity a human face,
And Love, the human form divine,
And Peace, the human dress.

Then every man, of every clime,
That prays in his distress,
Prays to the human form divine,
Love, Mercy, Pity, Peace.

And all must love the human form,
In heathen, turk, or jew;
Where Mercy, Love, & Pity dwell
There God is dwelling too.
William Blake

JERUSALEM

And did those feet in ancient time
Walk upon England's mountains green?
And was the holy Lamb of God
On England's pleasant pastures seen?

And did the Countenance Divine
Shine forth upon our clouded hills?
And was Jerusalem builded here
Among these dark Satanic Mills?

Bring me my bow of burning gold!
Bring me my arrows of desire!
Bring me my spear! O clouds, unfold!
Bring me my chariot of fire!

I will not cease from mental fight,
Nor shall my sword sleep in my hand,
Till we have built Jerusalem
In England's green and pleasant land.

William Blake

HOLY THURSDAY

'Twas on a Holy Thursday, their innocent faces
    clean,
Came children walking two and two, in red, and
    blue, and green;
Gray-headed beadles walked before, with wands as
    white as snow,
Till into the high dome of Paul's they like Thames
    waters flow.

O what a multitude they seemed, these flowers of
    London town!
Seated in companies they sit, with radiance all their
    own;
The hum of multitudes was there, but multitudes of
    lambs,
Thousands of little boys and girls raising their
    innocent hands.

Now, like a mighty wind, they raise to heaven the
    voice of song,
Or like harmonious thunderings the seats of heaven
    among;
Beneath them sit the agèd men, wise guardians of
    the poor.
Then cherish pity, lest you drive an angel from your
    door.

William Blake

INFANT JOY

"I have no name:
I am but two days old."
What shall I call thee?
"I happy am,
Joy is my name."
Sweet joy befall thee!

Pretty joy!
Sweet joy but two days old,
Sweet joy I call thee:
Thou dost smile,
I sing the while,
Sweet joy befall thee!

William Blake

THE LAMB

Little lamb who made thee?
Dost thou know who made thee,
Gave thee life and bid thee feed
By the stream and o'er the mead;
Gave thee clothing of delight,
Softest clothing, woolly, bright;
Gave thee such a tender voice?
Making all the vales rejoice?
Little lamb who made thee?
Dost thou know who made thee?

Little lamb, I'll tell thee,
Little lamb, I'll tell thee.
He is callèd by thy name,
For He calls Himself a Lamb:
He is meek and He is mild,
He became a little child.
I a child and thou a lamb,
We are callèd by His name.
Little lamb, God bless thee,
Little lamb, God bless thee.

William Blake

ETERNITY

He who bends to himself a Joy
Doth the wingèd life destroy;
But he who kisses the Joy as it flies
Lives in Eternity's sunrise.

William Blake

A RED, RED ROSE

O my Luve's like a red, red rose
That's newly sprung in June:
O my Luve's like the melodie
That's sweetly play'd in tune.

As fair art thou, my bonnie lass,
So deep in luve am I:
And I will luve thee still, my dear,
Till a' the seas gang dry:

Till a' the seas gang dry, my dear,
And the rocks melt wi' the sun;
I will luve thee still, my dear,
While the sands o' life shall run.

And fare thee weel, my only Luve!
And fare thee weel a while!
And I will come again, my Luve,
Tho' it were ten thousand mile.

Robert Burns

JOHN ANDERSON

John Anderson my jo, John,
When we were first acquent
Your locks were like the raven,
Your bonnie brow was brent;
But now your brow is beld, John,
Your locks are like the snow;
But blessings on your frosty pow,
John Anderson my jo.

John Anderson my jo, John,
We clamb the hill thegither,
And mony a canty day, John,
We've had wi' ane anither:
Now we maun totter down, John,
But hand in hand we'll go,
And sleep thegither at the foot,
John Anderson my jo.

                      Robert Burns

THE 19 TH CENTURY: MAINLY ROMANTIC AND NATURE

LOCHINVAR

O young Lochinvar is come out of the west,
Through all the wide Border his steed was the best,
And save his good broad-sword he weapons had
  none;
He rode all unarmed, and he rode all alone.
So faithful in love, and so dauntless in war,
There never was knight like the young Lochinvar.

He stay'd not for brake, and he stopp'd not for stone,
He swam the Esk river where ford there was none;
But, ere he alighted at Netherby gate,
The bride had consented, the gallant came late:
For a laggard in love, and a dastard in war,
Was to wed the fair Ellen of brave Lochinvar.

So boldly he entered the Netherby Hall,
Among bride's-men and kinsmen, and brothers and
  all:
Then spoke the bride's father, his hand on his sword
(For the poor craven bridegroom said never a word),
"O come ye in peace here, or come ye in war,
Or to dance at our bridal, young Lord Lochinvar?"

"I long wooed your daughter, my suit you denied:—
Love swells like the Solway, but ebbs like its tide—
And now I am come, with this lost love of mine
To lead but one measure, drink one cup of wine.
There are maidens in Scotland more lovely by far
That would gladly be bride to the young Lochinvar."

The bride kiss'd the goblet; the knight took it up,
He quaff'd off the wine, and he threw down the cup;

She look'd down to blush, and she look'd up to sigh,
With a smile on her lips and a tear in her eye.
He took her soft hand, ere her mother could bar,—
"Now tread we a measure!" said young Lochinvar.

So stately his form, and so lovely her face,
That never a hall such a galliard did grace;
While her mother did fret, and her father did fume,
And the bridegroom stood dangling his bonnet and
   plume;
And the bride-maidens whisper'd, "'Twere better by
   far
To have match'd our fair cousin with young
   Lochinvar."

One touch to her hand, and one word in her ear,
When they reach'd the hall-door, and the charger
   stood near;
So light to the croupe the fair lady he swung,
So light to the saddle before her he sprung!
"She is won! we are gone, over bank, bush, and
   scaur;
They'll have fleet steeds that follow," quoth young
   Lochinvar.

There was mounting 'mong Graemes of the
   Netherby clan;
Forsters, Fenwicks, and Musgraves, they rode and
   they ran:
There was racing and chasing on Cannobie Lee,
But the lost bride of Netherby ne'er did they see.
So daring in love, and so dauntless in war,
Have ye e'er heard of gallant like young Lochinvar?

                                   Sir Walter Scott

DAFFODILS

I wander'd lonely as a cloud
That floats on high o'er vales and hills,
When all at once I saw a crowd,
A host, of golden daffodils;
Beside the lake, beneath the trees,
Fluttering and dancing in the breeze.

Continuous as the stars that shine
And twinkle on the Milky Way,
They stretch'd in never-ending line
Along the margin of a bay;
Ten thousand saw I at a glance,
Tossing their heads in sprightly dance.

The waves beside them danced; but they
Out-did the sparkling waves in glee:
A poet could not but be gay,
In such a jocund company:
I gazed—and gazed—but little thought
What wealth the show to me had brought:

For oft, when on my couch I lie
In vacant or in pensive mood,
They flash upon that inward eye
Which is the bliss of solitude;
And then my heart with pleasure fills,
And dances with the daffodils.

                              William Wordsworth

From INTIMATIONS OF IMMORTALITY FROM
RECOLLECTIONS OF
EARLY CHILDHOOD

Our birth is but a sleep and a forgetting;
The Soul that rises with us, our life's Star,
Hath had elsewhere its setting,
And cometh from afar;
Not in entire forgetfulness,
And not in utter nakedness,
But trailing clouds of glory do we come
From God, who is our home.
Heaven lies about us in our infancy!
Shades of the prison-house begin to close
Upon the growing Boy,
But he beholds the light, and whence it flows.
He sees it in his joy;
The Youth, who daily farther from the east
Must travel, still is Nature's priest,
And by the vision splendid
Is on his way attended;
At length the Man perceives it die away,
And fade into the light of common day.

O joy! that in our embers
Is something that doth live,
That Nature yet remembers
What was so fugitive!
The thought of our past years in me doth breed
Perpetual benediction: not indeed
For that which is most worthy to be blest,
Delight and liberty, the simple creed
Of Childhood, whether busy or at rest,
With new-fledged hope still fluttering in his breast:

—Not for these I raise
The song of thanks and praise;
But for those obstinate questionings
Of sense and outward things,
Fallings from us, vanishings,
Blank misgivings of a creature
Moving about in worlds not realized,
High instincts, before which our mortal nature
Did tremble like a guilty thing surprised:
But for those first affections,
Those shadowy recollections,
Which, be they what they may,
Are yet the fountain-light of all our day,
Are yet a master-light of all our seeing;
Uphold us, cherish, and have power to make
Our noisy years seem moments in the being
Of the eternal silence: truths that wake,
To perish never;
Which neither listlessness, nor mad endeavour,
Nor Man nor Boy
Nor all that is at enmity with joy,
Can utterly abolish or destroy!
Hence in a season of calm weather
Though inland far we be,
Our souls have sight of that immortal sea
Which brought us hither;
Can in a moment travel thither—
And see the children sport upon the shore,
And hear the mighty waters rolling evermore.
William Wordsworth

UPON WESTMINSTER BRIDGE

Earth has not anything to show more fair:
Dull would he be of soul who could pass by
A sight so touching in its majesty:
This City now doth like a garment wear
The beauty of the morning; silent, bare,
Ships, towers, domes, theatres, and temples lie
Open unto the fields, and to the sky;
All bright and glittering in the smokeless air.
Never did sun more beautifully steep
In his first splendour, valley, rock, or hill;
Ne'er saw I, never felt, a calm so deep!
The river glideth at his own sweet will:
Dear God! the very houses seem asleep;
And all that mighty heart is lying still!

William Wordsworth

SMALL SERVICE

Small service is true service while it lasts;
Of friends, however humble, scorn not one:
The daisy by the shadow that it casts
Protects the lingering dew-drop from the sun.

William Wordsworth

KUBLA KHAN

In Xanadu did Kubla Khan
A stately pleasure-dome decree:
Where Alph, the sacred river, ran
Through caverns measureless to man
Down to a sunless sea.
So twice five miles of fertile ground
With walls and towers were girdled round:
And there were gardens bright with sinuous rills,
Where blossomed many an incense-bearing tree;
And here were forests ancient as the hills,
Enfolding sunny spots of greenery.

But oh! that deep romantic chasm which slanted
Down the green hill athwart a cedarn cover!
A savage place! as holy and enchanted
As e'er beneath a waning moon was haunted
By woman wailing for her demon-lover!
And from this chasm, with ceaseless turmoil
    seething,
As if this Earth in fast thick pants were breathing,
A mighty fountain momently was forced:
Amid whose swift half-intermitted burst
Huge fragments vaulted like rebounding hail,
Or chaffy grain beneath the thresher's flail:
And 'mid these dancing rocks at once and ever
It flung up momently the sacred river.
Five miles meandering with a mazy motion
Through wood and dale the sacred river ran,
Then reached the caverns measureless to man,
And sank in tumult to a lifeless ocean:
And 'mid this tumult Kubla heard from far
Ancestral voices prophesying war!

9—B.H.

The shadow of the dome of pleasure
Floated midway on the waves;
Where was heard the mingled measure
From the fountain and the caves.
It was a miracle of rare device,
A sunny pleasure-dome with caves of ice!

A damsel with a dulcimer
In a vision once I saw:
It was an Abyssinian maid,
And on her dulcimer she play'd,
Singing of Mount Abora.
Could I revive within me
Her symphony and song,
To such a deep delight 'twould win me
That with music loud and long,
I would build that dome in air,
That sunny dome! those caves of ice!
And all who heard should see them there,
And all should cry, Beware! Beware!
His flashing eyes, his floating hair!
Weave a circle round him thrice,
And close your eyes with holy dread,
For he on honey-dew hath fed,
And drunk the milk of Paradise.

Samuel Taylor Coleridge

SWANS SING

Swans sing before they die—'twere no bad thing
Should certain persons die before they sing.

Samuel Taylor Coleridge

From ADONAIS: *on the death of Keats*

He is a portion of the loveliness
Which once he made more lovely: he doth bear
His part, while the one Spirit's plastic stress
Sweeps through the dull dense world, compelling
   there
All new successions to the forms they wear;
Torturing th'unwilling dross that checks its flight
To its own likeness, as each mass may bear;
And bursting in its beauty and its might
From trees and beasts and men into the Heaven's
   light.

The splendours of the firmament of time
May be eclipsed, but are extinguished not;
Like stars to their appointed height they climb
And death is a low mist which cannot blot
The brightness it may veil. When lofty thought
Lifts a young heart above its mortal lair,
And love and life contend in it, for what
Shall be its earthly doom, the dead live there
And move like winds of light on dark and stormy
   air . . .

The One remains, the many change and pass;
Heaven's light forever shines, Earth's shadows fly;
Life, like a dome of many-coloured glass,
Stains the white radiance of Eternity,
Until Death tramples it to fragments.—Die,
If thou would'st be with that which thou dost seek!
Follow where all is fled!—Rome's azure sky,
Flowers, ruins, statues, music, words, are weak
The glory they transfuse with fitting truth to speak.

The breath whose might I have invoked in song
Descends on me; my spirit's bark is driven,
Far from the shore, far from the trembling throng
Whose sails were never to the tempest given;
The massy earth and spherèd skies are riven!
I am borne darkly, fearfully, afar;
Whilst burning through the inmost veil of Heaven,
The soul of Adonais, like a star,
Beacons from the abode where the Eternal are.

Percy Bysshe Shelley

THE QUESTION

I dream'd that, as I wander'd by the way,
Bare Winter suddenly was changed to Spring;
And gentle odours led my steps astray,
Mix'd with a sound of waters murmuring
Along a shelving bank of turf, which lay
Under a copse, and hardly dared to fling
Its green arms round the bosom of the stream,
But kiss'd it and then fled, as thou mightest in
    dream.

There grew pied wind-flowers and violets;
Daisies, those pearl'd Arcturi of the earth,
The constellated flower that never sets;
Faint oxlips; tender bluebells, at whose birth
The sod scarce heaved; and that tall flower that
    wets—
Like a child, half in tenderness and mirth—
Its mother's face with heaven-collected tears
When the low wind, its playmate's voice, it hears.

And in the warm hedge grew lush eglantine,
Green cowbind and the moonlight-colour'd May,
And cherry-blossoms, and white cups whose wine
Was the bright dew yet drain'd not by the day;
And wild roses, and ivy serpentine,
With its dark buds and leaves wandering astray;
And flowers, azure, black, and streak'd with gold,
Fairer than any waken'd eyes behold.

And nearer to the river's trembling edge
There grew broad flag-flowers, purple prank'd with
   white,
And starry river-buds among the sedge,
And floating water-lilies, broad and bright,
Which lit the oak that overhung the hedge
With moonlight beams of their own watery light;
And bulrushes, and reeds of such deep green
As soothed the dazzled eye with sober sheen.

Methought that of these visionary flowers
I made a nosegay, bound in such a way
That the same hues which in their natural bowers
Were mingled or opposed, the like array
Kept these imprison'd children of the Hours
Within my hand;—and then, elate and gay,
I hasten'd to the spot whence I had come,
That I might there present it—O! to whom?

Percy Bysshe Shelley

TO NIGHT

Swiftly walk o'er the western wave,
Spirit of Night!
Out of the misty eastern cave,
Where, all the long and lone daylight,
Thou wovest dreams of joy and fear,
Which make thee terrible and dear,—
Swift be thy flight!

Wrap thy form in a mantle grey,
Star-inwrought!
Blind with thine hair the eyes of Day,
Kiss her until she be wearied out,
Then wander o'er city, and sea, and land,
Touching all with thine opiate wand—
Come, long-sought!

When I arose and saw the dawn,
I sighed for thee;
When light rode high, and the dew was gone,
And noon lay heavy on flower and tree,
And the weary Day turned to her rest,
Lingering like an unloved guest,
I sighed for thee.

Thy brother Death came, and cried,
Wouldst thou me?
Thy sweet child Sleep, the filmy-eyed,
Murmured like a noontide bee,
Shall I nestle near thy side?
Wouldst thou me?—And I replied,
No, not thee!

Death will come when thou art dead,
Soon, too soon—
Sleep will come when thou art fled;
Of neither would I ask the boon
I ask of thee, belovèd Night—
Swift be thine approaching flight,
Come soon, soon!

Percy Bysshe Shelley

A WIDOW BIRD

A widow bird sate mourning for her love
Upon a wintry bough;
The frozen wind crept on above,
The freezing stream below.

There was no leaf upon the forest bare,
No flower upon the ground,
And little motion in the air
Except the mill-wheel's sound.

Percy Bysshe Shelley

HYMN OF PAN

From the forests and highlands
We come, we come:
From the river-girt islands,
Where loud waves are dumb,
Listening to my sweet pipings.
The wind in the reeds and the rushes,
The bees on the bells of thyme,
The birds on the myrtle bushes,
The cicale above in the lime,

And the lizards below in the grass,
Were as silent as ever old Tmolus was,
Listening to my sweet pipings.

Liquid Peneus was flowing,
And all dark Tempe lay
In Pelion's shadow, outgrowing
The light of the dying day,
Speeded by my sweet pipings.
The Sileni, and Sylvans, and Fauns,
And the Nymphs of the woods and waves,
To the edge of the moist river-lawns,
And the brink of the dewy caves,
And all that did then attend and follow,
Were silent with love, as you now, Apollo,
With envy of my sweet pipings.

I sang of the dancing stars,
I sang of the daedal Earth,
And of Heaven—and the giant wars,
And Love, and Death, and Birth.
And then I changed my pipings,—
Singing how down the vale of Maenalus
I pursued a maiden and clasped a reed.
Gods and men, we are all deluded thus!
It breaks in our bosom and then we bleed.
All wept, as I think both ye now would,
If envy or age had not frozen your blood,
At the sorrow of my sweet pipings.
                              Percy Bysshe Shelley

ODE TO THE WEST WIND

O wild West Wind, thou breath of Autumn's being,
Thou, from whose unseen presence the leaves dead
Are driven, like ghosts from an enchanter fleeing,
Yellow, and black, and pale, and hectic red,
Pestilence-stricken multitudes: O thou
Who chariotest to their dark wintry bed
The wingèd seeds, where they lie cold and low,
Each like a corpse within its grave, until
Thine azure sister of the Spring shall blow
Her clarion o'er the dreaming earth, and fill
(Driving sweet buds like flocks to feed in air)
With living hues and odours plain and hill:
Wild Spirit, which art moving everywhere;
Destroyer and Preserver; hear, oh, hear!

Thou on whose stream, 'mid the steep sky's
　　commotion,
Loose clouds like earth's decaying leaves are shed,
Shook from the tangled boughs of Heaven and
　　Ocean,
Angels of rain and lightning; there are spread
On the blue surface of thine airy surge,
Like the bright hair uplifted from the head
Of some fierce Mænad, ev'n from the dim verge
Of the horizon to the zenith's height—
The locks of the approaching storm. Thou dirge
Of the dying year, to which this closing night
Will be the dome of a vast sepulchre,
Vaulted with all thy congregated might
Of vapours, from whose solid atmosphere
Black rain, and fire, and hail, will burst; oh, hear!

Thou who didst waken from his summer-dreams
The blue Mediterranean, where he lay,
Lull'd by the coil of his crystàlline streams,
Beside a pumice isle in Baiae's bay,
And saw in sleep old palaces and towers
Quivering within the wave's intenser day,
All overgrown with azure moss and flowers
So sweet, the sense faints picturing them! Thou
For whose path the Atlantic's level powers
Cleave themselves into chasms, while far below
The sea-blooms and the oozy woods which wear
The sapless foliage of the ocean, know
Thy voice, and suddenly grow grey with fear
And tremble and despoil themselves: oh, hear!

If I were a dead leaf thou mightest bear;
If I were a swift cloud to fly with thee;
A wave to pant beneath thy power, and share
The impulse of thy strength, only less free
Than thou, O uncontrollable! If even
I were as in my boyhood, and could be
The comrade of thy wanderings over heaven,
As then, when to outstrip thy skiey speed
Scarce seem'd a vision, I would ne'er have striven
As thus with thee in prayer in my sore need.
Oh, lift me as a wave, a leaf, a cloud!
I fall upon the thorns of life! I bleed!
A heavy weight of hours has chain'd and bow'd
One too like thee: tameless, and swift, and proud.

Make me thy lyre, ev'n as the forest is:
What if my leaves are falling like its own!
The tumult of thy mighty harmonies
Will take from both a deep autumnal tone,

Sweet though in sadness. Be thou, Spirit fierce,
My spirit! be thou me, impetuous one!
Drive my dead thoughts over the universe
Like wither'd leaves to quicken a new birth;
And, by the incantation of this verse,
Scatter, as from an unextinguish'd hearth
Ashes and sparks, my words among mankind!
Be through my lips to unawaken'd earth
The trumpet of a prophecy! O Wind,
If Winter comes, can Spring be far behind?

Percy Bysshe Shelley

A LAMENT

O World! O Life! O Time!
On whose last steps I climb,
Trembling at that where I had stood before;
When will return the glory of your prime?
No more—Oh, never more!

Out of the day and night
A joy has taken flight:
Fresh spring, and summer, and winter hoar
Move my faint heart with grief, but with delight
No more—Oh, never more!

Percy Bysshe Shelley

ODE TO A NIGHTINGALE

My heart aches, and a drowsy numbness pains
My sense, as though of hemlock I had drunk,
Or emptied some dull opiate to the drains
One minute past, and Lethe-wards had sunk:
'Tis not through envy of thy happy lot,
But being too happy in thy happiness,—
That thou, light-wingèd Dryad of the trees,
In some melodious plot
Of beechen green, and shadows numberless,
Singest of summer in full-throated ease.

O for a draught of vintage! that hath been
Cooled a long age in the deep-delvèd earth,
Tasting of Flora and the country–green,
Dance, and Provençal song, and sunburnt mirth!
O for a beaker full of the warm South,
Full of the true, the blushful Hippocrene,
With beaded bubbles winking at the brim,
And purple-stainèd mouth;
That I might drink, and leave the world unseen,
And with thee fade away into the forest dim:

Fade far away, dissolve, and quite forget
What thou among the leaves hast never known,
The weariness, the fever, and the fret
Here, where men sit and hear each other groan:
Where palsy shakes a few, sad, last grey hairs,
Where youth grows pale, and spectre-thin, and dies;
Where but to think is to be full of sorrow
And leaden-eyed despairs;
Where Beauty cannot keep her lustrous eyes,
Or new Love pine at them beyond to-morrow.

Away! away! for I will fly to thee,
Not charioted by Bacchus and his pards,
But on the viewless wings of Poesy,
Though the dull brain perplexes and retards:
Already with thee! tender is the night,
And haply the Queen-Moon is on her throne,
Clustered around by all her starry Fays;
But here there is no light,
Save what from heaven is with the breezes blown
Through verdurous glooms and winding mossy
    ways.

I cannot see what flowers are at my feet,
Nor what soft incense hangs upon the boughs,
But, in embalmèd darkness, guess each sweet
Wherewith the seasonable month endows
The grass, the thicket, and the fruit-tree wild;
White hawthorn, and the pastoral eglantine;
Fast-fading violets covered up in leaves;
And mid-May's eldest child,
The coming musk-rose, full of dewy wine,
The murmurous haunt of flies on summer eves.

Darkling I listen; and for many a time
I have been half in love with easeful Death,
Called him soft names in many a musèd rhyme,
To take into the air my quiet breath;
Now more than ever seems it rich to die,
To cease upon the midnight with no pain,
While thou art pouring forth thy soul abroad
In such an ecstasy!
Still wouldst thou sing, and I have ears in vain—
To thy high requiem become a sod.

Thou wast not born for death, immortal Bird!
No hungry generations tread thee down;
The voice I hear this passing night was heard
In ancient days by emperor and clown:
Perhaps the self-same song that found a path
Through the sad heart of Ruth, when, sick for home,
She stood in tears amid the alien corn;
The same that oft-times hath
Charm'd magic casements, opening on the foam
Of perilous seas, in faery lands forlorn.

Forlorn! the very word is like a bell
To toll me back from thee to my sole self!
Adieu! the Fancy cannot cheat so well
As she is famed to do, deceiving elf.
Adieu! adieu! thy plaintive anthem fades
Past the near meadows, over the still stream,
Up the hill-side; and now 'tis buried deep
In the next valley-glades:
Was it a vision or a waking dream?
Fled is that music:—Do I wake or sleep?

John Keats

ODE ON A GRECIAN URN

Thou still unravish'd bride of quietness,
Thou foster-child of silence and slow time,
Sylvan historian, who canst thus express
A flowery tale more sweetly than our rhyme;
What leaf-fring'd legend haunts about thy shape
Of deities or mortals, or of both,
In Tempe or the dales of Arcady?
What men or gods are these? What maidens loth?
What mad pursuit? What struggle to escape?
What pipes and timbrels? What wild ecstasy?

Heard melodies are sweet, but those unheard
Are sweeter; therefore, ye soft pipes, play on;
Not to the sensual ear, but, more endear'd,
Pipe to the spirit ditties of no tone:
Fair youth beneath the trees, thou canst not leave
Thy song, nor ever can those trees be bare;
Bold Lover, never, never canst thou kiss,
Though winning near the goal—yet, do not grieve;
She cannot fade, though thou hast not thy bliss,
For ever wilt thou love, and she be fair!

Ah, happy, happy boughs! that cannot shed
Your leaves, nor ever bid the Spring adieu;
And, happy melodist, unwearièd,
For ever piping songs for ever new;
More happy love! more happy, happy love!
For ever warm and still to be enjoy'd,
For ever panting, and for ever young;
All breathing human passion far above,
That leaves a heart high-sorrowful and cloy'd,
A burning forehead, and a parching tongue.

Who are these coming to the sacrifice?
To what green altar, O mysterious priest,
Lead'st thou that heifer lowing at the skies,
And all her silken flanks with garlands drest?
What little town by river or sea shore,
Or mountain-built with peaceful citadel,
Is emptied of its folk, this pious morn?
And, little town, thy streets for evermore
Will silent be; and not a soul to tell
Why thou art desolate, can e'er return.

O Attic shape! Fair attitude! with brede
Of marble men and maidens overwrought,
With forest branches and the trodden weed;
Thou, silent form, dost tease us out of thought
As doth eternity: Cold Pastoral!
When old age shall this generation waste,
Thou shalt remain, in midst of other woe
Than ours, a friend to man, to whom thou say'st,
"Beauty is truth, truth beauty,"—that is all
Ye know on earth, and all ye need to know.

John Keats

ODE TO AUTUMN

Season of mists and mellow fruitfulness,
Close bosom-friend of the maturing sun;
Conspiring with him how to load and bless
With fruit the vines that round the thatch-eaves run;
To bend with apples the moss'd cottage-trees,
And fill all fruit with ripeness to the core;
To swell the gourd, and plump the hazel shells
With a sweet kernel; to set budding more,
And still more, later flowers for the bees,
Until they think warm days will never cease,
For summer has o'erbrimm'd their clammy cells.

Who hath not seen thee oft amid thy store?
Sometimes whoever seeks abroad may find
Thee sitting careless on a granary floor,
Thy hair soft-lifted by the winnowing wind;
Or on a half-reap'd furrow sound asleep,
Drows'd with the fume of poppies, while thy hook
Spares the next swath and all its twinèd flowers;

And sometimes like a gleaner thou dost keep
Steady thy laden head across a brook;
Or by a cider-press, with patient look,
Thou watchest the last oozings, hours by hours.

Where are the songs of Spring? Aye, where are they?
Think not of them,—thou hast thy music too,
While barrèd clouds bloom the soft-dying day
And touch the stubble-plains with rosy hue;
Then in a wailful choir the small gnats mourn
Among the river sallows, borne aloft
Or sinking as the light wind lives or dies;
And full-grown lambs loud bleat from hilly bourn;
Hedge-crickets sing, and now with treble soft
The redbreast whistles from a garden-croft,
And gathering swallows twitter in the skies.

John Keats

LA BELLE DAME SANS MERCI

"O what can ail thee, knight-at-arms,
Alone and palely loitering?
The sedge has wither'd from the Lake,
And no birds sing.

"O what can ail thee, knight-at-arms,
So haggard and so woebegone?
The squirrel's granary is full,
And the harvest's done.

"I see a lily on thy brow
With anguish moist and fever dew,
And on thy cheeks a fading rose
Fast withereth too."

"I met a Lady in the Meads,
Full beautiful—a faery's child,
Her hair was long, her foot was light,
And her eyes were wild.

"I made a garland for her head,
And bracelets too, and fragrant zone;
She look'd at me as she did love,
And made sweet moan.

"I set her on my pacing steed
And nothing else saw all day long,
For sidelong would she bend, and sing
A faery's song.

"She found me roots of relish sweet,
And honey wild and manna dew,
And sure in language strange she said,
'I love thee true.'

"She took me to her elfin grot,
And there she wept, and sigh'd full sore,
And there I shut her wild, wild eyes
With kisses four.

"And there she lullèd me asleep,
And there I dream'd—Ah! woe betide!
The latest dream I ever dream'd
On the cold hill's side.

"I saw pale Kings and Princes too,
Pale warriors, death-pale were they all;
They cried—'La belle Dame sans Merci
Hath thee in thrall!'

"I saw their starved lips in the gloam
With horrid warning gapèd wide,
And I awoke and found me here
On the cold hill's side.

"And this is why I sojourn here
Alone and palely loitering,
Though the sedge is wither'd from the Lake
And no birds sing."

John Keats

AFTER BLENHEIM

It was a summer evening,
Old Kaspar's work was done,
And he before his cottage door
Was sitting in the sun;
And by him sported on the green
His little grandchild Wilhelmine.

She saw her brother Peterkin
Roll something large and round
Which he beside the rivulet
In playing there had found;
He came to ask what he had found
That was so large and smooth and round.

Old Kaspar took it from the boy
Who stood expectant by;
And then the old man shook his head,
And with a natural sigh
"'Tis some poor fellow's skull," said he,
"Who fell in the great victory.

"I find them in the garden,
For there's many here about;
And often when I go to plough
The ploughshare turns them out.
For many thousand men," said he,
"Were slain in that great victory."

"Now tell us what 'twas all about,"
Young Peterkin he cries;
And little Wilhelmine looks up
With wonder-waiting eyes;
"Now tell us all about the war,
And what they fought each other for."

"It was the English," Kaspar cried,
"Who put the French to rout;
But what they fought each other for
I could not well make out.
But everybody said," quoth he,
"That 'twas a famous victory.

"My father lived at Blenheim then,
Yon little stream hard by;
They burnt his dwelling to the ground,
And he was forced to fly:
So with his wife and child he fled,
Nor had he where to rest his head.

"With fire and sword the country round
Was wasted far and wide,
And many a childing mother then
And new-born baby died:
But things like that, you know, must be
At every famous victory.

"They say it was a shocking sight
After the field was won;
For many thousand bodies here
Lay rotting in the sun:
But things like that, you know, must be
After a famous victory.

"Great praise the Duke of Marlbro' won
And our good Prince Eugene;"
"Why, 'twas a very wicked thing!"
Said little Wilhelmine;
"Nay . . . nay . . . my little girl," quoth he,
"It was a famous victory.

"And everybody praised the Duke
Who this great fight did win."
"But what good came of it at last?"
Quoth little Peterkin:—
"Why, that I cannot tell," said he,
"But 'twas a famous victory."

Robert Southey

DIRCE

Stand close around, ye Stygian set,
With Dirce in one boat conveyed,
Or Charon, seeing, may forget
That he is old and she a shade.

Walter Savage Landor

DEATH STANDS ABOVE ME

Death stands above me, whispering low
I know not what into my ear:
Of his strange language all I know
Is, there is not a word of fear.

Walter Savage Landor

I STROVE WITH NONE

I strove with none; for none was worth my strife.
Nature I loved and, next to Nature, Art;
I warmed both hands before the fire of life;
It sinks, and I am ready to depart.

Walter Savage Landor

ELGIN CATHEDRAL EPITAPH

Here lie I, Martin Elginbrodde:
Ha'e mercy o' my soul, Lord God,
As I wad do, were I Lord God
And ye were Martin Elginbrodde.

Anonymous

SUFFOLK EPITAPH

Stranger pass by and waste no time
On bad biography and careless rhyme.
For what I am, this humble stone encloses;
And what I was is no affair of yourses.

Anonymous

ABOU BEN ADHEM

Abou Ben Adhem (may his tribe increase!)
Awoke one night from a deep dream of peace,
And saw, within the moonlight in his room,
Making it rich, and like a lily in bloom,
An angel writing in a book of gold.
Exceeding peace had made Ben Adhem bold,
And to the presence in the room he said,
"What writest thou?"—The vision rais'd its head,
And with a look made all of sweet accord,
Answer'd, "The names of those that love the Lord".
"And is mine one?" said Abou. "Nay, not so,"
Replied the angel. Abou spoke more low,
But cheerly still; and said, "I pray thee, then,
Write me as one that loves his fellow men".
The angel wrote, and vanished. The next night
It came again with a great wakening light,
And show'd the names whom love of God had blest,
And lo! Ben Adhem's name led all the rest.

Leigh Hunt

JENNY KISS'D ME

Jenny kiss'd me when we met,
Jumping from the chair she sat in;
Time, you thief, who love to get
Sweets into your list, put that in!
Say I'm weary, say I'm sad,
Say that health and wealth have miss'd me,
Say I'm growing old, but add
Jenny kiss'd me.

Leigh Hunt

THE MINSTREL BOY

The Minstrel Boy to the war is gone,
In the ranks of death you'll find him;
His father's sword he has girded on,
And his wild harp slung behind him.
"Land of song!" said the warrior-bard,
"Though all the world betrays thee,
One sword, at least, thy rights shall guard,
One faithful harp shall praise thee!"

The Minstrel fell!—but the foeman's chain
Could not bring his proud soul under;
The harp he loved ne'er spoke again,
For he tore its chords asunder;
And said, "No chains shall sully thee,
Thou soul of love and bravery!
Thy songs were made for the pure and free:
They shall never sound in slavery!"

Thomas Moore

DESTRUCTION OF SENNACHERIB

The Assyrian came down like the wolf on the fold,
And his cohorts were gleaming in purple and gold;
And the sheen of their spears was like stars on the
    sea,
When the blue wave rolls nightly on deep Galilee.

Like the leaves of the forest when Summer is green,
That host with their banners at sunset were seen:
Like the leaves of the forest when Autumn hath
    blown,
That host on the morrow lay wither'd and strown.

For the Angel of Death spread his wings on the blast,
And breathed in the face of the foe as he pass'd;
And the eyes of the sleepers wax'd deadly and chill,
And their hearts but once heaved, and for ever grew
    still!

And there lay the steed with his nostril all wide,
But through it there roll'd not the breath of his
    pride;
And the foam of his gasping lay white on the turf,
And cold as the spray of the rock-beating surf.

And there lay the rider distorted and pale,
With the dew on his brow, and the rust on his mail:
And the tents were all silent, the banners alone,
The lances unlifted, the trumpet unblown.

And the widows of Ashur are loud in their wail
And the idols are broke in the temple of Baal;
And the might of the Gentile, unsmote by the
    sword,
Hath melted like snow in the glance of the Lord!

Lord Byron

From THE ISLES OF GREECE

The isles of Greece! The isles of Greece
Where burning Sappho loved and sung,
Where grew the arts of war and peace,
Where Delos rose, and Phoebus sprung!
Eternal summer gilds them yet,
But all, except their sun, is set.

The mountains look on Marathon—
And Marathon looks on the sea;
And musing there an hour alone,
I dream'd that Greece might still be free;
For, standing on the Persians' grave,
I could not deem myself a slave.

A king sate on the rocky brow
Which looks o'er sea-born Salamis;
And ships, by thousands, lay below,
And men in nations;—all were his!
He counted them at break of day—
And when the sun set, where were they?

And where are they? and where art thou,
My country? On thy voiceless shore
The heroic lay is tuneless now—
The heroic bosom beats no more!
And must thy lyre, so long divine,
Degenerate into hands like mine?

Must we but weep o'er days more blest?
Must we but blush?—Our fathers bled.
Earth! render back from out thy breast
A remnant of our Spartan dead!
Of the three hundred grant but three,
To make a new Thermopylae!

Lord Byron

WE'LL GO NO MORE A-ROVING

So, we'll go no more a-roving
So late into the night,
Though the heart be still as loving,
And the moon be still as bright.

For the sword outwears its sheath,
And the soul wears out the breast,
And the heart must pause to breathe,
And love itself have rest.

Though the night was made for loving,
And the day returns too soon,
Yet we'll go no more a-roving
By the light of the moon.

Lord Byron

THE BURIAL OF SIR JOHN MOORE
AFTER CORUNNA

Not a drum was heard, not a funeral note,
As his corse to the rampart we hurried;
Not a soldier discharged his farewell shot
O'er the grave where our hero we buried.

We buried him darkly at dead of night,
The sods with our bayonets turning;
By the struggling moonbeam's misty light,
And the lantern dimly burning.

No useless coffin enclosed his breast,
Not in sheet or in shroud we wound him;
But he lay like a warrior taking his rest,
With his martial cloak around him.

Few and short were the prayers we said,
And we spoke not a word of sorrow;
But we steadfastly gazed on the face that was dead,
And we bitterly thought of the morrow.

We thought, as we hollowed his narrow bed,
And smoothed down his lonely pillow,
That the foe and the stranger would tread o'er his
   head,
And we far away on the billow!

Lightly they'll talk of the spirit that's gone,
And o'er his cold ashes upbraid him,—
But little he'll reck, if they let him sleep on
In the grave where a Briton has laid him.

But half of our heavy task was done
When the clock struck the hour for retiring;
And we heard the distant and random gun
That the foe was sullenly firing.

Slowly and sadly we laid him down,
From the field of his fame fresh and gory;
We carved not a line, and we raised not a stone—
But we left him alone with his glory.

Charles Wolfe

THE THRUSH'S NEST

Within a thick and spreading hawthorn bush,
That overhung a molehill large and round,
I heard from morn to eve a merry thrush
Sing hymns to sunrise, and I drank the sound
With joy; and often, an intruding guest,
I watched her secret toil from day to day—
How true she warped the moss, to form a nest,
And modelled it within with wood and clay;
And by-and-by, like heath-bells gilt with dew,
There lay her shining eggs, as bright as flowers,
Ink-spotted over shells of greeny blue;
And there I witnessed in the sunny hours
A brood of Nature's minstrels chirp and fly,
Glad as the sunshine and the laughing sky.

John Clare

THE MOTHER'S DREAM

I'd a dream to-night
As I fell asleep,
Oh! the touching sight
Makes me still to weep—
Of my little lad,
Gone to leave me sad,
Aye, the child I had,
But was not to keep.

As in heaven high,
I my child did seek,
There, in train, came by
Children fair and meek,

Each in lily white,
With a lamp alight;
Each was clear to sight,
But they did not speak.

Then, a little sad,
Came my child in turn,
But the lamp he had,
Oh! it did not burn;
He, to clear my doubt,
Said, half turned about,
"Your tears put it out;
Mother, never mourn."

William Barnes

BRAHMA

If the red slayer think he slays,
Or if the slain think he is slain,
They know not well the subtle ways
I keep, and pass, and turn again.

Far or forgot to me is near;
Shadow and sunlight are the same;
The vanished gods to me appear;
And one to me are shame and fame.

They reckon ill who leave me out;
When me they fly, I am the wings;
I am the doubter and the doubt,
And I the hymn the Brahmin sings.

The strong gods pine for my abode,
And pine in vain the sacred Seven;
But thou, meek lover of the good!
Find me, and turn thy back on heaven.

Ralph Waldo Emerson

SONNET TO A MONKEY

O lively, O most charming pug,
Thy graceful air, and heavenly mug;
The beauties of his mind do shine,
And every bit is shaped and fine.
Your teeth are whiter than the snow,
You're a great buck, you're a great beau;
Your eyes are of so nice a shape,
More like a Christian's than an ape;
Your cheek is like the rose's blume,
Your hair is like the raven's plume;
His nose's cast is of the Roman,
He is a very pretty woman.
I could not get a rhyme for Roman,
So was obliged to call him woman.

Marjorie Fleming (ætat: 8)

GO FROM ME

Go from me. Yet I feel that I shall stand
Henceforward in thy shadow. Nevermore
Alone upon the threshold of my door
Of individual life, I shall command
The uses of my soul, nor lift my hand
Serenely in the sunshine as before,
Without the sense of that which I forbore—
Thy touch upon the palm. The widest land
Doom takes to part us, leaves thy heart in mine
With pulses that beat double. What I do
And what I dream include thee, as the wine
Must taste of its own grapes. And when I sue
God for myself, He hears that name of thine,
And sees within my eyes the tears of two.

Elizabeth Barrett Browning

IF THOU MUST LOVE ME

If thou must love me, let it be for naught
Except for love's sake only. Do not say,
"I love her for her smile—her look—her way
Of speaking gently,—for a trick of thought
That falls in well with mine, and certes brought
A sense of pleasant ease on such a day"—
For these things in themselves, Belovèd, may
Be changed, or change for thee—and love, so
   wrought,
May be unwrought so. Neither love me for
Thine own dear pity's wiping my cheeks dry:
A creature might forget to weep, who bore
Thy comfort long, and lose thy love thereby!
But love me for love's sake, that evermore
Thou mayst love on, through love's eternity.

Elizabeth Barrett Browning

A MUSICAL INSTRUMENT

What was he doing, the great god Pan,
Down in the reeds by the river?
Spreading ruin and scattering ban,
Splashing and paddling with hoofs of a goat,
And breaking the golden lilies afloat
With the dragon-fly on the river.

He tore out a reed, the great god Pan,
From the deep cool bed of the river;
The limpid water turbidly ran,
And the broken lilies a-dying lay,
And the dragon-fly had fled away,
Ere he brought it out of the river.

High on the shore sat the great god Pan,
While turbidly flow'd the river;
And hack'd and hew'd as a great god can
With his hard bleak steel at the patient reed,
Till there was not a sign of the leaf indeed
To prove it fresh from the river.

He cut it short, did the great god Pan
(How tall it stood in the river!)
Then drew the pith, like the heart of a man,
Steadily, from the outside ring,
And notch'd the poor dry empty thing
In holes, as he sat by the river.

"This is the way," laugh'd the great god Pan
(Laugh'd while he sat by the river),
"The only way, since gods began
To make sweet music, they could succeed."
Then dropping his mouth to a hole in the reed,
He blew in power by the river.

Sweet, sweet, sweet, O Pan!
Piercing sweet by the river!
Blinding sweet, O great god Pan!
The sun on the hill forgot to die,
And the lilies revived, and the dragon-fly
Came back to dream on the river.

Yet half a beast is the great god Pan,
To laugh as he sits by the river,
Making a poet out of a man:
The true gods sigh for the cost and pain—
For the reed which grows nevermore again
As a reed with the reeds of the river.

Elizabeth Barrett Browning

THE SLAVE'S DREAM

Beside the ungather'd rice he lay,
His sickle in his hand;
His breast was bare, his matted hair
Was buried in the sand.
Again, in the mist and shadow of sleep,
He saw his Native Land.

Wide through the landscape of his dreams
The lordly Niger flowed;
Beneath the palm-trees on the plain
Once more a king he strode;
And heard the tinkling caravans
Descend the mountain-road.

He saw once more his dark-eyed queen
Among her children stand;
They clasp'd his neck, they kiss'd his cheeks,
They held him by the hand!—
A tear burst from the sleeper's lids
And fell into the sand.

And then at furious speed he rode
Along the Niger's bank;
His bridle reins were golden chains,
And, with a martial clank,
At each leap he could feel his scabbard of steel
Smiting his stallion's flank.

Before him, like a blood-red flag,
The bright flamingoes flew;
From morn till night he follow'd their flight,
O'er plains where the tamarind grew,
Till he saw the roofs of Caffre huts,
And the ocean rose to view.

At night he heard the lion roar,
And the hyena scream,
And the river-horse, as he crush'd the reeds
Beside some hidden stream;
And it pass'd, like a glorious roll of drums,
Through the triumph of his dream.

The forests, with their myriad tongues,
Shouted of Liberty;
And the blast of the Desert cried aloud,
With a voice so wild and free,
That he started in his sleep and smiled
At their tempestuous glee.

He did not feel the driver's whip,
Nor the burning heat of day;
For Death had illumined the Land of Sleep,
And his lifeless body lay
A worn-out fetter, that the soul
Had broken and thrown away!

Henry Wadsworth Longfellow

STARS OF THE SUMMER NIGHT

Stars of the summer night!
Far in yon azure deeps,
Hide, hide your golden light!
She sleeps!
My lady sleeps!
Sleeps!

Moon of the summer night!
Far down yon western steeps,
Sink, sink in silver light!
She sleeps!
My lady sleeps!
Sleeps!

Wind of the summer night!
Where yonder woodbine creeps,
Fold, fold thy pinions light!
She sleeps!
My lady sleeps!
Sleeps!

Dreams of the summer night!
Tell her her lover keeps
Watch! while in slumbers light
She sleeps!
My lady sleeps!
Sleeps!

Henry Wadsworth Longfellow

From THE RUBÁIYÁT OF OMAR KHAYYÁM

Awake! for Morning in the Bowl of Night
Has flung the Stone that puts the Stars to Flight:
And Lo! the Hunter of the East has caught
The Sultan's Turret in a Noose of Light.

Dreaming when Dawn's Left Hand was in the Sky
I heard a Voice within the Tavern cry:
"Awake, my Little ones, and fill the Cup
Before Life's Liquor in its Cup be dry."

And, as the Cock crew, those who stood before
The Tavern shouted: "Open then the Door!
You know how little while we have to stay,
And, once departed, may return no more."

Here with a Loaf of Bread beneath the Bough,
A Flask of Wine, a Book of Verse—and Thou
Beside me singing in the Wilderness—
And Wilderness is Paradise enow.

Some for the Glories of This World; and some
Sigh for the Prophet's Paradise to come;
Ah, take the Cash, and let the Credit go,
Nor heed the rumble of a distant Drum!

Think, in this batter'd Caravanserai
Whose Portals are alternate Night and Day,
How Sultan after Sultan with his Pomp
Abode his destin'd Hour, and went his way.

Myself when young did eagerly frequent
Doctor and Saint, and heard great argument
About it and about: but evermore
Came out by the same door as in I went.

With them the seed of Wisdom did I sow,
And with mine own hand wrought to make it
  grow;
And this was all the Harvest that I reap'd:
"I came like Water, and like Wind I go."

The Moving Finger writes; and, having writ,
Moves on: nor all your Piety nor Wit
Shall lure it back to cancel half a Line,
Nor all your Tears wash out a Word of it.

                    Translated by Edward FitzGerald

TO HELEN

Helen, thy beauty is to me
Like those Nicèan barks of yore
That gently, o'er a perfumed sea,
The weary way-worn wanderer bore
To his own native shore.

On desperate seas long wont to roam,
Thy hyacinth hair, thy classic face,
Thy Naiad airs have brought me home
To the glory that was Greece,
And the grandeur that was Rome.

Lo, in yon brilliant window-niche
How statue-like I see thee stand,
The agate lamp within thy hand,
Ah! Psyche, from the regions which
Are holy land!

Edgar Allan Poe

ANNABEL LEE

It was many and many a year ago,
In a kingdom by the sea,
That a maiden there lived whom you may know
By the name of Annabel Lee.
And this maiden she lived with no other thought
Than to love and be loved by me.

I was a child and she was a child
In this kingdom by the sea:
But we loved with a love that was more than love
I and my Annabel Lee,
With a love that the wingèd seraphs of heaven
Coveted her and me.

And this was the reason that, long ago,
In this kingdom by the sea,
A wind blew out of a cloud, chilling
My beautiful Annabel Lee,
So that her high-born kinsman came
And bore her away from me,
To shut her up in a sepulchre
In this kingdom by the sea.

The angels, not half so happy in heaven,
Went envying her and me—
Yes! that was the reason (as all men know,
In this kingdom by the sea)
That the wind came out of the cloud one night,
Chilling and killing my Annabel Lee.

But our love it was stronger by far than the love
Of those who were older than we—
Of many far wiser than we—
And neither the angels in heaven above,
Nor the demons down under the sea,
Can ever dissever my soul from the soul
Of the beautiful Annabel Lee:

For the moon never beams without bringing me
    dreams
Of the beautiful Annabel Lee;
And the stars never rise, but I feel the bright eyes
Of the beautiful Annabel Lee;
And so, all the night-tide, I lie down by the side
Of my darling—my darling—my life and my bride.
In the sepulchre there by the sea,
In her tomb by the sounding sea.

Edgar Allan Poe

THE EAGLE

He clasps the crag with crooked hands;
Close to the sun in lonely lands,
Ringed with the azure world, he stands.

The wrinkled sea beneath him crawls;
He watches from his mountain walls,
And like a thunderbolt he falls.

Alfred, Lord Tennyson

SONG from THE BROOK

I come from haunts of coot and hern,
I make a sudden sally
And sparkle out among the fern,
To bicker down a valley.

By thirty hills I hurry down,
Or slip between the ridges,
By twenty thorps, a little town,
And half a hundred bridges.

Till last by Philip's farm I flow
To join the brimming river,
For men may come and men may go,
But I go on for ever.

I chatter over stony ways
In little sharps and trebles,
I bubble into eddying bays,
I babble on the pebbles.

With many a curve my banks I fret
By many a field and fallow,
And many a fairy-foreland set
With willow-weed and mallow.

I chatter, chatter, as I flow
To join the brimming river,
For men may come and men may go,
But I go on for ever.

I wind about, and in and out,
With here a blossom sailing,
And here and there a lusty trout,
And here and there a grayling,

And here and there a foamy flake
Upon me, as I travel
With many a silvery waterbreak
Above the golden gravel,

And draw them all along, and flow
To join the brimming river,
For men may come and men may go,
But I go on for ever.

I steal by lawns and grassy plots,
I slide by hazel covers;
I move the sweet forget-me-nots
That grow for happy lovers.

I slip, I slide, I gloom, I glance,
Among my skimming swallows;
I make the netted sunbeam dance
Against my sandy shallows.

I murmur under moon and stars
In brambly wildernesses;
I linger by my shingly bars;
I loiter round my cresses;

And out again I curve and flow
To join the brimming river,
For men may come and men may go,
But I go on for ever.

Alfred, Lord Tennyson

SONG from THE PRINCESS

The splendour falls on castle walls
And snowy summits old in story:
The long light shakes across the lakes,
And the wild cataract leaps in glory.
Blow, bugle, blow, set the wild echoes flying,
Blow, bugle; answer, echoes, dying, dying, dying.

O hark, O hear! how thin and clear,
And thinner, clearer, farther going!
O sweet and far from cliff and scar
The horns of Elfland faintly blowing!
Blow, let us hear the purple glens replying:
Blow, bugle; answer, echoes, dying, dying, dying.

O love, they die in yon rich sky,
They faint on hill or field or river:
Our echoes roll from soul to soul,
And grow for ever and for ever.
Blow, bugle, blow, set the wild echoes flying,
And answer, echoes, answer, dying, dying, dying.

Alfred, Lord Tennyson

From IN MEMORIAM

Be near me when my light is low,
When the blood creeps, and the nerves prick
And tingle; and the heart is sick,
And all the wheels of Being slow.

Be near me when the sensuous frame
Is rack'd with pangs that conquer trust;
And Time, a maniac scattering dust,
And Life, a Fury slinging flame.

Be near me when my faith is dry,
And men the flies of latter spring,
That lay their eggs, and sting and sing
And weave their petty cells and die.

Be near me when I fade away,
To point the term of human strife,
And on the low dark verge of life
The twilight of eternal day.

* * *

When Lazarus left his charnel-cave,
And home to Mary's house return'd,
Was this demanded—if he yearn'd
To hear her weeping by his grave?

"Where wert thou, brother, those four days?"
There lives no record of reply,
Which telling what it is to die
Had surely added praise to praise.

From every house the neighbours met,
The streets were fill'd with joyful sound,
A solemn gladness even crown'd
The purple brows of Olivet.

Behold a man raised up by Christ!
The rest remaineth unreveal'd;
He told it not; or something seal'd
The lips of that Evangelist.

* * *

Ring out, wild bells, to the wild sky,
The flying cloud, the frosty light:
The year is dying in the night;
Ring out, wild bells, and let him die.

Ring out the old, ring in the new,
Ring, happy bells, across the snow:
The year is going, let him go;
Ring out the false, ring in the true.

Ring out the grief that saps the mind,
For those that here we see no more;
Ring out the feud of rich and poor,
Ring in redress to all mankind.

Ring out a slowly dying cause,
And ancient forms of party strife;
Ring in the nobler modes of life,
With sweeter manners, purer laws.

Ring out the want, the care, the sin,
The faithless coldness of the times;
Ring out, ring out my mournful rhymes,
But ring the fuller minstrel in.

Ring out false pride in place and blood,
The civic slander and the spite;
Ring in the love of truth and right,
Ring in the common love of good.

Ring out old shapes of foul disease;
Ring out the narrowing lust of gold;
Ring out the thousand wars of old,
Ring in the thousand years of peace.

Ring in the valiant man and free,
The larger heart, the kindlier hand;
Ring out the darkness of the land,
Ring in the Christ that is to be.

Alfred, Lord Tennyson

HOW THEY BROUGHT THE GOOD NEWS FROM GHENT TO AIX

I sprang to the stirrup, and Joris, and he;
I galloped, Dirck galloped, we galloped all three;
"God speed!" cried the watch, as the gatebolts
    undrew;
"Speed!" echoed the wall to us galloping through;
Behind shut the postern, the lights sank to rest,
And into the midnight we galloped abreast.

Not a word to each other; we kept the great pace
Neck by neck, stride by stride, never changing our
    place;
I turned in my saddle and made its girths tight,
Then shortened each stirrup, and set the pique right,
Rebuckled the cheek-strap, chained slacker the bit,
Nor galloped less steadily Roland a whit.

'Twas moonset at starting; but while we drew near
Lokeren, the cocks crew and twilight dawned clear;
At Boom, a great yellow star came out to see;
At Düffeld, 'twas morning as plain as could be;
And from Mecheln church-steeple we heard the
   half-chime,
So, Joris broke silence with, "Yet there is time!"

At Aershot, up leaped of a sudden the sun,
And against him the cattle stood black every one,
To stare thro' the mist at us galloping past,
And I saw my stout galloper Roland at last,
With resolute shoulders, each butting away
The haze, as some bluff river headland its spray:

And his low head and crest, just one sharp ear bent
   back
For my voice, and the other pricked out on his track;
And one eye's black intelligence,—ever that glance
O'er its white edge at me, his own master, askance!
And the thick heavy spume-flakes which aye and
   anon
His fierce lips shook upwards in galloping on.

By Hasselt, Dirck groaned; and cried Joris, "Stay
   spur!
Your Roos galloped bravely, the fault's not in her,
We'll remember at Aix"—for one heard the quick
   wheeze
Of her chest, saw the stretched neck and staggering
   knees,
And sunk tail, and horrible heave of the flank,
As down on her haunches she shuddered and sank.

So, we were left galloping, Joris and I,
Past Looz and past Tongres, no cloud in the sky;
The broad sun above laughed a pitiless laugh,
'Neath our feet broke the brittle bright stubble like
  chaff;
Till over by Dalhem a dome-spire sprang white,
And "Gallop," gasped Joris, "for Aix is in sight!

"How they'll greet us!"—and all in a moment his
  roan
Rolled neck and croup over, lay dead as a stone;
And there was my Roland to bear the whole weight
Of the news which alone could save Aix from her
  fate,
With his nostrils like pits full of blood to the brim,
And with circles of red for his eye-sockets' rim.

Then I cast loose my buffcoat, each holster let fall,
Shook off both my jack-boots, let go belt and all,
Stood up in the stirrup, leaned, patted his ear,
Called my Roland his pet-name, my horse without
  peer;
Clapped my hands, laughed and sang, any noise, bad
  or good,
Till at length into Aix Roland galloped and stood.

And all I remember is—friends flocking round
As I sat with his head 'twixt my knees on the ground;
And no voice but was praising this Roland of mine,
As I poured down his throat our last measure of
  wine,
Which (the burgesses voted by common consent)
Was no more than his due who brought good news
  from Ghent.   Robert Browning

THE PATRIOT

It was roses, roses, all the way,
With myrtle mixed in my path like mad:
The house-roofs seemed to heave and sway,
The church-spires flamed, such flags they had,
A year ago on this very day.

The air broke into a mist with bells,
The old walls rocked with the crowd and cries.
Had I said, "Good folk, mere noise repels—
But give me your sun from yonder skies!"
They had answered, "And afterward, what else?"

Alack, it was I who leaped at the sun
To give it my loving friends to keep!
Nought man could do, have I left undone:
And you see my harvest, what I reap
This very day, now a year is run.

There's nobody on the house-tops now—
Just a palsied few at the windows set;
For the best of the sight is, all allow,
At the Shambles' Gate—or, better yet,
By the very scaffold's foot, I trow.

I go in the rain, and, more than needs,
A rope cuts both my wrists behind;
And I think, by the feel, my forehead bleeds,
For they fling, whoever has a mind,
Stones at me for my year's misdeeds.

Thus I entered, and thus I go!
In triumphs, people have dropped down dead.
"Paid by the world, what dost thou owe
Me?"—God might question; now instead,
'Tis God shall repay: I am safer so.

Robert Browning

HOME-THOUGHTS FROM ABROAD

Oh, to be in England
Now that April's there,
And whoever wakes in England
Sees, some morning, unaware,
That the lowest boughs and the brushwood sheaf
Round the elm-tree bole are in tiny leaf,
While the chaffinch sings on the orchard bough
In England—now!

And after April, when May follows,
And the whitethroat builds, and all the swallows!
Hark, where my blossom'd pear-tree in the hedge
Leans to the field and scatters on the clover
Blossoms and dewdrops—at the bent spray's edge—
That's the wise thrush; he sings each song twice over,
Lest you should think he never could recapture
The first fine careless rapture!
And though the fields look rough with hoary dew,
All will be gay when noontide wakes anew
The buttercups, the little children's dower
—Far brighter than this gaudy melon-flower!

Robert Browning

12—B.H.

PARTING AT MORNING

Round the cape of a sudden came the sea,
And the sun looked over the mountain's rim:
And straight was a path of gold for him,
And the need of a world of men for me.

Robert Browning

THE OWL AND THE PUSSY-CAT

The Owl and the Pussy-cat went to sea
In a beautiful pea-green boat,
They took some honey, and plenty of money,
Wrapped up in a five-pound note.
The Owl looked up to the stars above,
And sang to a small guitar,
"O lovely Pussy! O Pussy, my love,
What a beautiful Pussy you are,
You are
You are!
What a beautiful Pussy you are!"

Pussy said to the Owl, "You elegant fowl!
How charmingly sweet you sing!
O let us be married! too long we have tarried:
But what shall we do for a ring?"
They sailed away, for a year and a day,
To the land where the Bong-tree grows
And there in a wood a Piggy-wig stood
With a ring at the end of his nose,
His nose,
His nose,
With a ring at the end of his nose.

"Dear Pig, are you willing to sell for one shilling
Your ring?" Said the Piggy, "I will."
So they took it away, and were married next day
By the Turkey who lives on the hill.
They dined on mince, and slices of quince,
Which they ate with a runcible spoon;
And hand in hand, on the edge of the sand,
They danced by the light of the moon,
The moon,
The moon,
They danced by the light of the moon.

Edward Lear

From THE PRISONER

"Still let my tyrants know, I am not doom'd to wear
Year after year in gloom and desolate despair;
A messenger of Hope comes every night to me,
And offers for short life, eternal liberty.

"He comes with western winds, with evening's
    wandering airs,
With that clear dusk of heaven that brings the
    thickest stars;
Winds take a pensive tone and stars a tender fire
And visions rise and change which kill me with
    desire—

"Desire for nothing known in my maturer years
When joy grew mad with awe at counting future
    tears;
When, if my spirit's sky was full of flashes warm,
I knew not whence they came, from sun or thunder-
    storm;

"But first a hush of peace, a soundless calm descends;
The struggle of distress and fierce impatience ends;
Mute music soothes my breast—unuttered harmony
That I could never dream till earth was lost to me.

"Then dawns the Invisible, the Unseen its truth
    reveals;
My outward sense is gone, my inward essence feels—
Its wings are almost free, its home, its harbour
    found;
Measuring the gulf it stoops and dares the final
    bound!

"Oh dreadful is the check—intense the agony
When the ear begins to hear and the eye begins to
    see;
When the pulse begins to throb, the brain to think
    again;
The soul to feel the flesh and the flesh to feel the
    chain!"

Emily Brontë

LAST LINES

No coward soul is mine,
No trembler in the world's storm-troubled sphere:
I see Heaven's glories shine,
And faith shines equal, arming me from fear.

O God within my breast,
Almighty, ever-present Deity!
Life—that in me has rest,
As I—undying Life—have power in Thee!

Vain are the thousand creeds
That move men's hearts: unutterably vain;
Worthless as wither'd weeds,
Or idlest froth amid the boundless main,

To waken doubt in one
Holding so fast by Thine infinity;
So surely anchor'd on
The steadfast rock of immortality.

With wide-embracing love
Thy Spirit animates eternal years,
Pervades and broods above,
Changes, sustains, dissolves, creates, and rears.

Though earth and man were gone,
And suns and universes cease to be,
And Thou were left alone,
Every existence would exist in Thee.

There is not room for Death,
Nor atom that his might could render void:
Thou—Thou art Being and Breath,
And what Thou art may never be destroyed.

Emily Brontë

THE LAST WORD

Creep into thy narrow bed,
Creep, and let no more be said!
Vain thy onset! all stands fast.
Thou thyself must break at last.

Let the long contention cease!
Geese are swans, and swans are geese,
Let them have it how they will!
Thou art tired; best be still!

They out-talked thee, hissed thee, tore thee?
Better men fared thus before thee;
Fired their ringing shot and passed,
Hotly charged—and sank at last.

Charge once more, then, and be dumb!
Let the victors, when they come,
When the forts of folly fall,
Find thy body by the wall!

Matthew Arnold

MAGNA EST VERITAS

Here, in this little Bay,
Full of tumultuous life and great repose,
Where, twice a day,
The purposeless, glad ocean comes and goes,
Under high cliffs, and far from the huge town,
I sit me down.
For want of me the world's course will not fail:
When all its work is done, the lie shall rot;
The truth is great, and shall prevail,
When none cares whether it prevail or not.

Coventry Patmore

A FAREWELL

With all my will, but much against my heart,
We two now part.
My Very Dear,
Our solace is, the sad road lies so clear.
It needs no art,
With faint, averted feet
And many a tear,
In our opposèd paths to persevere.
Go thou to East, I West.
We will not say
There's any hope, it is so far away.
But, O my Best,
When the one darling of our widowhead,
The nursling Grief,
Is dead,
And no dews blur our eyes
To see the peach-bloom come in evening skies,
Perchance we may,
Where now this night is day,
And even through faith of still averted feet,
Making full circle of our banishment,
Amazèd meet;
The bitter journey to the bourne so sweet
Seasoning the termless feast of our content
With tears of recognition never dry.

Coventry Patmore

THE KISS

"I saw you take his kiss!" "'Tis true,"
"O, modesty!" "'Twas strictly kept:
He thought me asleep: at least, I knew
He thought I thought he thought I slept."

Coventry Patmore

THE TOYS

My little Son, who look'd from thoughtful eyes,
And moved and spoke in quiet grown-up wise,
Having my law the seventh time disobey'd,
I struck him, and dismiss'd
With hard words and unkiss'd,
His mother, who was patient, being dead.
Then, fearing lest his grief should hinder sleep,
I visited his bed,
But found him slumbering deep,
With darken'd eyelids, and their lashes yet
From his late sobbing wet.
And I, with moan,
Kissing away his tears, left others of my own;
For, on a table drawn beside his head,
He had put within his reach,
A box of counters and a red-veined stone,
A piece of glass abraded by the beach,
And six or seven shells,
A bottle with bluebells,
And two French copper coins, ranged there with
  careful art
To comfort his sad heart.
So when that night I pray'd
To God, I wept, and said:
Ah, when at last we lie with trancèd breath,
Not vexing Thee in death,
And thou rememberest of what toys
We made our joys,
How weakly understood
Thy great commanded good,
Then, fatherly not less

Than I whom Thou hast moulded from the clay,
Thou'lt leave Thy wrath, and say
"I will be sorry for their childishness."

Coventry Patmore

From MODERN LOVE

We saw the swallows gathering in the sky,
And in the osier-isle we heard them noise.
We had not to look back on summer joys,
Or forward to a summer of bright dye:
But in the largeness of the evening earth
Our spirits grew as we went side by side.
The hour became her husband and my bride.
Love that had robbed us so, thus blessed our dearth!
The pilgrims of the year waxed very loud
In multitudinous chatterings, as the flood
Full brown came from the West, and like pale blood
Expanded to the upper crimson cloud.
Love that had robbed us of immortal things
This little moment mercifully gave,
Where I have seen across the twilight wave
The swan sail with her young beneath her wings.

George Meredith

LUCIFER IN STARLIGHT

On a starr'd night Prince Lucifer uprose.
Tired of his dark dominion swung the fiend
Above the rolling ball in cloud part screen'd,
Where sinners hugg'd their spectre of repose.
Poor prey to his hot fit of pride were those.
And now upon his western wing he lean'd,
Now his huge bulk o'er Afric's sands careen'd,
Now the black planet shadow'd Arctic snows.

Soaring through wider zones that prick'd his scars
With memory of the old revolt from Awe,
He reach'd a middle height, and at the stars,
Which are the brain of heaven, he look'd, and sank.
Around the ancient track march'd, rank on rank,
The army of unalterable law.

George Meredith

VESPERS

O blackbird, what a boy you are!
How you do go it!
Blowing your bugle to that one sweet star—
How you do blow it!
And does she hear you, blackbird boy, so far?
Or is it wasted breath?
"Good Lord, she is so bright
To-night!"
The blackbird saith.

T. E. Brown

THE LILY-POOL AND THE COW

What sees our mailie in the lily-pool,
What sees she with that large surprise?
What sees our mailie in the lily-pool
With all the violet of her big eyes—
Our mailie in the lily-pool?

She sees herself within the lily-pool,
Herself in flakes of brown and white—
Herself beneath the slab that is the lily-pool,
The green and liquid slab of light
With cups of silver dight,

Stem-rooted in the depths of amber night
That hold the hollows of the lily-pool—
Our own dear lily-pool!

And does she gaze into the lily-pool
As one that is enchanted?
Or does she try the cause to find
How the reflection's slanted,
That sleeps within the lily-pool?
Or does she take it all for granted
With the sweet natural logic of her kind?
The lazy logic of the lily-pool,
Our own bright, innocent, stupid lily-pool!

She knows that it is nice—our lily-pool:
She likes the water-rings around her knees;
She likes the shadow of the trees,
That droop above the lily-pool;
She likes to scatter with a silly sneeze
The long-legged flies that skim the lily-pool—
The peaceful-sleeping, baby lily-pool.

So may I look upon the lily-pool,
Nor ever in the slightest care
Why I am there;
Why upon land and sea
Is ever stamped the inevitable me;
But rather say with that most gentle fool—
"How pleasant is this lily-pool!
How nice and cool!
Be off, you long-legged flies! O what a spree!
To drive the flies from off the lily-pool!
From off this most sufficient, absolute lily-pool!"

T. E. Brown

THE WOODSPURGE

The wind flapped loose, the wind was still,
Shaken out dead from tree and hill;
I had walk'd on at the wind's will,—
I sat now, for the wind was still.

Between my knees my forehead was,—
My lips, drawn in, said not Alas:
My hair was over in the grass,
My naked ears heard the day pass.

My eyes, wide open, had the run
Of some ten weeds to fix upon;
Among those few, out of the sun,
The woodspurge flowered, three cups in one.

From perfect grief there need not be
Wisdom or even memory:
One thing then learnt remains to me,—
The woodspurge has a cup of three.

Dante Gabriel Rossetti

LOST DAYS

The lost days of my life until to-day,
What were they, could I see them on the street
Lie as they fell? Would they be ears of wheat
Sown once for food but trodden into clay?
Or golden coins squandered and still to pay?
Or drops of blood dabbling the guilty feet?
Or such spilt water as in dreams must cheat
The undying throats of Hell, athirst alway?

I do not see them here; but after death
God knows I know the faces I shall see,
Each one a murdered self, with low last breath,
"I am thyself,—what hast thou done to me?
And I—and I—thyself," (lo! each one saith),
"And thou thyself to all eternity!"

Dante Gabriel Rossetti

LIFE

I asked no other thing,
No other was denied.
I offered Being for it;
The mighty merchant smiled.

Brazil? He twirled a button,
Without a glance my way:
"But, madam, is there nothing else
That we can show to-day?"

Emily Dickinson

MY LIFE CLOSED TWICE

My life closed twice before its close;
It yet remains to see
If Immortality unveil
A third event to me,

So huge, so hopeless to conceive,
As these that twice befell.
Parting is all we know of Heaven,
And all we need of hell.

Emily Dickinson

THE SHOW

The show is not the show,
But they that go.
Menagerie to me
My neighbours be.
Fair play—
Both went to see.

Emily Dickinson

UPHILL

Does the road wind uphill all the way?
   Yes, to the very end.
Will the day's journey take the whole long day?
   From morn to night, my friend.

But is there for the night a resting-place?
   A roof for when the slow dark hours begin.
May not the darkness hide it from my face?
   You cannot miss that inn.

Shall I meet other wayfarers at night?
   Those who have gone before.
Then must I knock, or call when just in sight?
   They will not keep you waiting at that door.

Shall I find comfort, travel-sore and weak?
   Of labour you shall find the sum.
Will there be beds for me and all who seek?
   Yea, beds for all who come.

Christina Rossetti

SONG

When I am dead, my dearest,
Sing no sad songs for me;
Plant thou no roses at my head,
Nor shady cypress tree:
Be the green grass above me
With showers and dewdrops wet:
And if thou wilt, remember,
And if thou wilt, forget.

I shall not see the shadows,
I shall not feel the rain;
I shall not hear the nightingale
Sing on as if in pain:
And dreaming through the twilight
That doth not rise nor set,
Haply I may remember,
And haply may forget.

Christina Rossetti

THE PHASES OF THE MOON

O Lady Moon, your horns point to the East;
Shine, be increased!
O Lady Moon, your horns point to the West;
Wane, be at rest!

Christina Rossetti

REMEMBER

Remember me when I am gone away,
Gone far away into the silent land;
When you can no more hold me by the hand,
Nor I half turn to go, yet turning stay.
Remember me when no more day by day
You tell me of our future that you plann'd:
Only remember me; you understand
It will be late to counsel then or pray.
Yet if you should forget me for a while
And afterwards remember, do not grieve:
For if the darkness and corruption leave
A vestige of the thoughts that once I had,
Better by far you should forget and smile
Than that you should remember and be sad.

Christina Rossetti

AT GLASTONBURY

Magdalen at Michael's gate
Tirlèd at the pin;
On Joseph's thorn sang the blackbird,
"Let her in! Let her in!"

"Hast thou seen the wounds?" said Michael,
"Knowest thou thy sin?"
"It is evening, evening," sang the blackbird,
"Let her in! Let her in!"

"Yes I have seen the wounds,
And I know my sin."
"She knows it well, well, well," sang the blackbird,
"Let her in! Let her in!"

"Thou bringest no offerings," said Michael,
"Nought save sin."
And the blackbird sang "She is sorry, sorry, sorry.
Let her in! Let her in!"

When he had sung himself to sleep,
And night did begin,
One came and opened Michael's gate,
And Magdalen went in.

Henry Kingsley

From THE SCHOOLMASTER ABROAD WITH HIS SON

Oh, what harper could worthily harp it,
Mine Edward! this wide-stretching wold
(Look out *wold*) with its wonderful carpet
Of emerald, purple, and gold?
Look well at it—also look sharp, it
Is getting so cold.

The purple is heather (*erica*);
The yellow gorse—call'd sometimes "whin".
Cruel boys on its prickles might spike a
Queen beetle as if on a pin.
You may ride in it, if you would like a
Few holes in your skin.

You wouldn't? Then think of how kind you
Should be to the insects who crave
Your compassion—and then look behind you
At yon barley-ears! Don't they look brave
As they undulate (*undulate*, mind you,
From *unda*, a wave).

13—B.H.

Then yon desolate eerie morasses
The haunt of the snipe and the hern—
(I shall question the two upper classes
On *aquatiles* when we return)—
Why, I see on them absolute masses
Of *felix*, or fern.

How it interests e'en a beginner
(Or *tiro*) like dear little Ned!
Is he listening? As I am a sinner,
He's asleep—he is wagging his head.
Wake up! I'll go home to my dinner,
And you to your bed.

Charles Stuart Calverley

From SYLVIE AND BRUNO

He thought he saw an Elephant,
That practised on a fife:
He looked again, and found it was
A letter from his wife.
"At length I realize," he said,
"The bitterness of Life!"

He thought he saw a Buffalo
Upon the chimney-piece:
He looked again, and found it was
His Sister's Husband's Niece,
"Unless you leave this house," he said,
"I'll send for the Police!"

He thought he saw a Rattlesnake
That questioned him in Greek:
He looked again, and found it was
The Middle of Next Week.
"The one thing I regret," he said,
"Is that it cannot speak!"

He thought he saw a Banker's Clerk
Descending from the bus:
He looked again, and found it was
A Hippopotamus:
"If this should stay to dine," he said,
"There won't be much for us!"

Lewis Carroll

From QUESTIONS OF THE HOUR

"How old is God? Has He grey hair?
Can He see yet? Where did He have to stay
Before—you know—He had made—Anywhere?
Who does He pray to—when He has to pray?

"How many drops are in the sea?
How many stars?—well, then, you ought to know
How many flowers are on an apple-tree?
How does the wind look when it doesn't blow?"

S. M. B. Piatt

I HEARD A LINNET COURTING

I heard a linnet courting
His lady in the spring:
His mates were idly sporting,
Nor stayed to hear him sing
His song of love.—
I fear my speech distorting
His tender love.

The phrases of his pleading
Were full of young delight;
And she that gave him heeding
Interpreted aright
His gay, sweet notes,—
So sadly marred in the reading,—
His tender notes.

And when he ceased, the hearer
Awaited the refrain,
Till swiftly perching nearer
He sang his song again,
His pretty song:—
Would that my verse spake clearer
His tender song!

Ye happy, airy creatures!
That in the merry spring
Think not of what misfeatures
Or cares the year may bring;
But unto love
Resign your simple natures
To tender love.

Robert Bridges

THE IDLE LIFE I LEAD

The idle life I lead
Is like a pleasant sleep,
Wherein I rest and heed
The dreams that by me sweep.

And still of all my dreams
In turn so swiftly past,
Each in its fancy seems
A nobler than the last.

And every eve I say,
Noting my step in bliss,
That I have known no day
In all my life like this.

Robert Bridges

I LOVE ALL BEAUTEOUS THINGS

I love all beauteous things,
I seek and adore them;
God hath no better praise,
And man in his hasty days
Is honoured for them.

I too will something make
And joy in the making;
Altho' to-morrow it seem
Like the empty words of a dream
Remembered on waking.

Robert Bridges

WEATHERS

This is the weather the cuckoo likes,
And so do I;
When showers betumble the chestnut spikes,
And nestlings fly;
And the little brown nightingale bills his best,
And they sit outside the "Traveller's Rest",
And maids come forth sprig-muslin drest,
And citizens dream of the South and West,
And so do I.

This is the weather the shepherd shuns,
And so do I:
When beeches drip in browns and duns,
And thresh, and ply;
And hill-hid tides throb, throe on throe,
And meadow rivulets overflow,
And drops on gate-bars hang in a row,
And rooks in families homeward go,
And so do I.

Thomas Hardy

HEAVEN-HAVEN: *A Nun Takes the Veil*

I have desired to go
Where springs not fail,
To fields where flies no sharp and sided hail
And a few lilies blow.

And I have asked to be
Where no storms come,
Where the green swell is in the havens dumb,
And out of the swing of the sea.

Gerard Manley Hopkins

PIED BEAUTY

Glory be to God for dappled things—
For skies of couple-colour as a brinded cow;
For rose-moles all in stipple upon trout that swim;
Fresh-firecoal chestnut-falls; finches' wings;
Landscape plotted and pieced—fold, fallow, and
    plough;
And áll trádes, their gear and tackle and trim.

All things counter, original, spare, strange;
Whatever is fickle, freckled (who knows how?)
With swift, slow; sweet, sour; adazzle, dim;
He fathers-forth whose beauty is past change:
Praise him.

Gerard Manley Hopkins

THE RAINY SUMMER

There's much afoot in heaven and earth this year;
The winds hunt up the sun, hunt up the moon,
Trouble the dubious dawn, hasten the drear
Height of a threatening noon.

No breath of boughs, no breath of leaves, of fronds,
May linger or grow warm; the trees are loud;
The forest, rooted, tosses in her bonds,
And strains against the cloud.

No scents may pause within the garden-fold;
The rifled flowers are cold as ocean-shells;
Bees, humming in the storm, carry their cold
Wild honey to cold cells.

Alice Meynell

From CHRIST IN THE UNIVERSE

With this ambiguous earth
His dealings have been told us. These abide:
The signal to a maid, the human birth,
The lesson, and the young Man crucified.

But not a star of all
The innumerable host of stars has heard
How He administered this terrestrial ball.
Our race have kept their Lord's entrusted Word.

No planet knows that this
Our wayside planet, carrying land and wave,
Love and life multiplied, and pain and bliss,
Bears, as chief treasure, one forsaken grave.

Nor, in our little day,
May His devices with the heavens be guessed,
His pilgrimage to thread the Milky Way,
Or His bestowals there be manifest.

But, in the eternities,
Doubtless we shall compare together, hear
A million alien Gospels, in what guise
He trod the Pleiades, the Lyre, the Bear.

O be prepared, my soul!
To read the inconceivable, to scan
The million forms of God those stars unroll
When, in our turn, we show to them a Man.

Alice Meynell

THE WIND IS BLIND
"Eyeless, in Gaza, at the mill, with slaves"—
  Milton's *Samson*

The wind is blind.
The earth sees sun and moon; the height
Is watch-tower to the dawn; the plain
Shines to the summer; visible light
Is scattered in the drops of rain.

The wind is blind.
The flashing billows are aware;
With open eyes the cities see;
Light leaves the ether, everywhere
Known to the homing bird and bee.

The wind is blind,
Is blind alone. How has he hurled
His ignorant lash, his aimless dart,
His eyeless rush, upon the world,
Unseeing, to break his unknown heart!

The wind is blind,
And the sail traps him, and the mill
Captures him; and he cannot save
His swiftness and his desperate will
From those blind uses of the slave.

Alice Meynell

THE COURTS
A Figure of the Epiphany

The poet's imageries are noble ways,
Approaches to a plot, an open shrine,
Their spendours, colours, avenues, arrays,
Their courts that run with wine;

Beautiful similes, "fair and flagrant things,"
Enriched, enamouring,—raptures, metaphors
Enhancing life, are paths for pilgrim kings
Made free of golden doors.

And yet the open heavenward plot, with dew,
Ultimate poetry, enclosed, enskied,
(Albeit such ceremonies lead thereto)
Stands on the yonder side.

Plain, behind oracles, it is; and past
All symbols, simple; perfect, heavenly-wild,
The song some loaded poets reach at last—
The kings that found a Child.

                                        Alice Meynell

ENVOY

Go, little book, and wish to all
Flowers in the garden, meat in the hall,
A bin of wine, a spice of wit,
A house with lawns enclosing it,
A living river by the door,
A nightingale in the sycamore!

                                Robert Louis Stevenson

THE CELESTIAL SURGEON

If I have faltered more or less
In my great task of happiness;
If I have moved among my race
And shown no glorious morning face;
If beams from happy human eyes
Have moved me not; if morning skies,
Books, and my food, and summer rain
Knocked on my sullen heart in vain:
Lord, thy most pointed pleasure take
And stab my spirit broad awake;
Or, Lord, if too obdurate I,
Choose thou, before that spirit die,
A piercing pain, a killing sin,
And to my dead heart run them in!

Robert Louis Stevenson

SING ME A SONG

Sing me a song of a lad that is gone,
Say, could that lad be I?
Merry of soul he sailed on a day
Over the sea to Skye.

Mull was astern, Rum on the port,
Eigg on the starboard bow;
Glory of youth glowed in his soul:
Where is that glory now?

Sing me a song of a lad that is gone,
Say, could that lad be I?
Merry of soul he sailed on a day
Over the sea to Skye.

Give me again all that was there,
Give me the sun that shone!
Give me the eyes, give me the soul,
Give me the lad that's gone!

Sing me a song of a lad that is gone,
Say, could that lad be I?
Merry of soul he sailed on a day
Over the sea to Skye.

Billow and breeze, islands and seas,
Mountains of rain and sun,
All that was good, all that was fair,
All that was me is gone.

Robert Louis Stevenson

IN THE HIGHLANDS

In the highlands, in the country places,
Where the old plain men have rosy faces,
And the young fair maidens
Quiet eyes;
Where essential silence cheers and blesses,
And for ever in the hill-recesses
Her more lovely music
Broods and dies.

O to mount again where erst I haunted;
Where the old red hills are bird-enchanted,
And the low green meadows
Bright with sward;
And when even dies, the million-tinted,
And the night has come, and planets glinted,
Lo, the valley hollow
Lamp-bestarred!

O to dream, O to awake and wander
There, and with delight to take and render,
Through the trance of silence,
Quiet breath;
Lo! for there, among the flowers and grasses,
Only the mightier movement sounds and passes;
Only winds and rivers,
Life and death.

Robert Louis Stevenson

THE FINE SONG FOR SINGING

I will make you brooches and toys for your delight
Of bird-song at morning and star-shine at night.
I will make a palace fit for you and me
Of green days in forests and blue days at sea.

I will make my kitchen, and you shall keep your
    room,
Where white flows the river and bright blows the
    broom,
And you shall wash your linen and keep your body
    white
In rainfall at morning and dewfall at night.

And this shall be for music when no one else is near,
The fine song for singing, the rare song to hear!
That only I remember, that only you admire,
Of the broad road that stretches and the roadside
    fire.

Robert Louis Stevenson

ON WENLOCK EDGE

On Wenlock Edge the wood's in trouble;
His forest fleece the Wrekin heaves;
The gale, it plies the saplings double,
And thick on Severn snow the leaves.

'Twould blow like this through holt and hanger
When Uricon the city stood:
'Tis the old wind in the old anger,
But then it threshed another wood.

Then, 'twas before my time, the Roman
At yonder heaving hill would stare:
The blood that warms an English yeoman,
The thoughts that hurt him, they were there.

There, like the wind through woods in riot,
Through him the gale of life blew high;
The tree of man was never quiet:
Then 'twas the Roman, now 'tis I.

The gale, it plies the saplings double,
It blows so hard, 'twill soon be gone:
To-day the Roman and his trouble
Are ashes under Uricon.

A. E. Housman

FROM FAR

From far, from eve and morning
And yon twelve-winded sky,
The stuff of life to knit me
Blew hither: here am I.

Now—for a breath I tarry
Nor yet disperse apart—
Take my hand quick and tell me,
What have you in your heart.

Speak now, and I will answer;
How shall I help you, say;
Ere to the wind's twelve quarters
I take my endless way.

A. E. Housman

ARAB LOVE SONG

The hunchèd camels of the night
Trouble the bright
And silver waters of the moon.
The Maiden of the Morn will soon
Through Heaven stray and sing,
Star gathering.
Now while the dark about our loves is strewn,
Light of my dark, blood of my heart, O come!
And night will catch her breath up, and be dumb.

Leave thy father, leave thy mother
And thy brother;
Leave the black tents of thy tribe apart!
Am I not thy father and thy brother,
And thy mother?
And thou—what needest with thy tribe's black tents
Who hast the red pavilion of my heart?

Francis Thompson

THE KINGDOM OF GOD
"In no Strange Land"

O world invisible, we view thee,
O world intangible, we touch thee,
O world unknowable, we know thee,
Inapprehensible, we clutch thee!

Does the fish soar to find the ocean,
The eagle plunge to find the air—
That we ask of the stars in motion
If they have rumour of thee there?

Not where the wheeling systems darken,
And our benumbed conceiving soars!—
The drift of pinions, would we hearken,
Beats at our own clay-shuttered doors.

The angels keep their ancient places;—
Turn but a stone, and start a wing!
'Tis ye, 'tis your estrangèd faces,
That miss the many-splendoured thing.

But (when so sad thou canst not sadder)
Cry;—and upon thy so sore loss
Shall shine the traffic of Jacob's ladder
Pitched betwixt Heaven and Charing Cross.

Yea, in the night, my Soul, my daughter,
Cry,—clinging Heaven by the hems;
And lo, Christ walking on the water
Not of Gennesareth, but Thames!

Francis Thompson

THE HEART

O nothing, in this corporal earth of man,
That to the imminent heaven of his high soul
Responds with colour and with shadow, can
Lack correlated greatness. If the scroll
Where thoughts lie fast in spell of hieroglyph
Be mighty through its mighty habitants;
If God be in His Name; grave potence if
The sounds unbind of hieratic chants:
All's vast that vastness means. Nay, I affirm
Nature is whole in her least things exprest,
Nor know we with what scope God builds the worm.
Our towns are copied fragments from our breast;
And all man's Babylons strive but to impart
The grandeurs of his Babylonian heart.

Francis Thompson

From AN ECHO OF VICTOR HUGO

Life's a veil the real has:
All the shadows of our scene
Are but shows of things that pass
On the other side the screen.

Time his glass sits nodding by;
'Twixt its turn and turn a spawn
Of universes buzz and die
Like the ephemeris of the dawn.

O our towered altitudes!
O the lustres of our thrones!
What! old Time shall have his moods
Like Caesars and Napoleons;

Have his towers and conquerors forth,
Till he, weary of the toys,
Put back Rameses in the earth
And break his Ninevehs and Troys.

Francis Thompson

AT LORD'S

It is little I repair to the matches of the Southron
    folk,
Though my own red roses there may blow;
It is little I repair to the matches of the Southron
    folk,
Though the red roses crest the caps, I know.
For the field is full of shades as I near the shadowy
    coast,
And a ghostly batsman plays to the bowling of a
    ghost,
And I look through my tears on a soundless-clapping
    host
As the run-stealers flicker to and fro,
To and fro:—
O my Hornby and my Barlow long ago!

Francis Thompson

WISHES AT A GARDEN PARTY

I wish I loved the Human Race;
I wish I loved its silly face;
I wish I liked the way it walks;
I wish I liked the way it talks;
And when I'm introduced to one
I wish I thought *What Jolly Fun!*

Walter Raleigh

THE WEAPON

The weapon that you fought with was a word,
And with that word you stabbed me to the heart.
Not once but twice you did it, for the sword
Made no blood start.

They have not tried you for your life. You go
Strong in such innocence as men will boast.
They have not buried me. They do not know
Life from its ghost.

Mary Coleridge

EGYPT'S MIGHT IS TUMBLED DOWN

Egypt's might is tumbled down
Down a-down the deeps of thought;
Greece is fallen and Troy town,
Glorious Rome hath lost her crown,
Venice' pride is nought.

But the dreams their children dreamed
Fleeting, unsubstantial, vain,
Shadowy as the shadows seemed,
Airy nothing, as they deemed,
These remain.

Mary Coleridge

THE INALIENABLE

Says Death: "I take your son." The Thief: "Your
  gold."
Says Fate: "I seize on all you have and hold."
"And I," the Slanderer says, "your name destroy."
"But who," the Poet asks, "can take my joy?"

Rabindranath Tagore

SLOW SPRING

O year, grow slowly. Exquisite, holy,
The days go on
With almonds showing the pink stars blowing,
And birds in the dawn.

Grow slowly, year, like a child that is dear,
Or a lamb that is mild,
By little steps, and by little skips,
Like a lamb or a child.

Katharine Tynan

YOU CAN'T PLEASE EVERYBODY

The Duke of Rutland urged *The Times* to pray
For rain: the rain came down the following day.
The pious marvelled: sceptics murmured: "Fluke!"
And farmers late with hay said: "Damn that Duke!"

Quoted by E. V. Lucas

DRAKE'S DRUM

Drake he's in his hammock an' a thousand mile
    away,
(Capten, art tha sleepin' there below?)
Slung atween the round shot in Nombre Dios Bay,
An' dreamin' arl the time o' Plymouth Hoe.
Yarnder lumes the Island, yarnder lie the ships,
Wi' sailor-lads a-dancin' heel-an'-toe,
An' the shore-lights flashin', an' the night-tide
    dashin',
He sees et arl so plainly as he saw et long ago.

Drake he was a Devon man, an' ruled the Devon
   seas,
(Capten, art tha sleepin' there below?)
Rovin' tho' his death fell, he went wi' heart at ease,
An' dreamin' arl the time o' Plymouth Hoe.
"Take my drum to England, hang et by the shore,
Strike et when your powder's runnin' low;
If the Dons sight Devon, I'll quit the port o' Heaven,
An' drum them up the Channel as we drummed
   them long ago!"

Drake he's in his hammock till the great Armadas
   come,
(Capten, art tha sleepin' there below?)
Slung atween the round shot, listenin' for the drum,
An' dreamin' arl the time o' Plymouth Hoe.
Call him on the deep sea, call him up the Sound,
Call him when ye sail to meet the foe;
Where the old trade's plyin' an' the old flag flyin'
They shall find him ware an' wakin', as they found
   him long ago!

Sir Henry Newbolt

WE ARE ALONE

We are alone: the dead who sleeping lie,
And I who mow the grass above their head.
Since I still move, I say: "The dead—and I,"
But had I thought of what it is to die,
And what to live, I might have simply said,
"We dead."

Anna Bunston de Bary

CITIES AND THRONES

Cities and Thrones and Powers
Stand in Time's eye,
Almost as long as flowers,
Which daily die:
But, as new buds put forth
To glad new men,
Out of the spent and unconsidered Earth
The Cities rise again.

This season's Daffodil,
She never hears
What change, what chance, what chill,
Cut down last year's;
But with bold countenance,
And knowledge small,
Esteems her seven days' continuance
To be perpetual.

So Time that is o'er-kind
To all that be,
Ordains us e'en as blind,
As bold as she:
That in our very death,
And burial sure,
Shadow to shadow, well persuaded, saith,
"See how our works endure!"

Rudyard Kipling

From THE LEGENDS OF EVIL

This is the sorrowful story
Told as the twilight fails
And the monkeys walk together
Holding their neighbours' tails:—

"Our fathers lived in the forest,
Foolish people were they,
They went down to the cornland
To teach the farmers to play.

"Our fathers frisked in the millet,
Our fathers skipped in the wheat;
Our fathers hung from the branches,
Our fathers danced in the street.

"Then came the terrible farmers,
Nothing of play they knew,
Only . . . they caught our fathers
And set them to labour too!

"Set them to work in the cornland
With ploughs and sickles and flails,
Put them in mud-walled prisons,
And—cut off their beautiful tails!

"Now, we can watch our fathers,
Sullen and bowed and old,
Stooping over the millet,
Sharing the silly mould;

"Driving a foolish furrow,
Mending a muddy yoke,
Sleeping in mud-walled prisons,
Steeping their food in smoke.

"We may not speak with our fathers,
For if the farmers knew
They would come up to the forest
And set us to labour too."

This is the horrible story
Told as the twilight fails
And the monkeys walk together
Holding their neighbours' tails.

Rudyard Kipling

THE PRECEPT OF SILENCE

I know you: solitary griefs,
Desolate passions, aching hours!
I know you: tremulous beliefs,
Agonized hopes, and ashen flowers!

The winds are sometimes sad to me;
The starry spaces, full of fear;
Mine is the sorrow on the sea,
And mine the sigh of places drear.

Some players upon plaintive strings
Publish their wistfulness abroad:
I have not spoken of these things,
Save to one man, and unto God.

Lionel Johnson

THE 20TH CENTURY: SENSE AND THE SENSES

THE SONG OF
WANDERING AENGUS

I went out to the hazel wood,
Because a fire was in my head,
And cut and peeled a hazel wand,
And hooked a berry to a thread;
And when white moths were on the wing,
And moth-like stars were flickering out,
I dropped the berry in a stream
And caught a little silver trout.

When I had laid it on the floor
I went to blow the fire aflame,
But something rustled on the floor,
And some one called me by my name:
It had become a glimmering girl
With apple blossom in her hair
Who called me by my name and ran
And faded through the brightening air.

Though I am old with wandering
Through hollow lands and hilly lands,
I will find out where she has gone,
And kiss her lips and take her hands;
And walk among long dappled grass,
And pluck till time and times are done
The silver apples of the moon,
The golden apples of the sun.

W. B. Yeats

WHEN YOU ARE OLD

When you are old and grey and full of sleep,
And nodding by the fire, take down this book,
And slowly read, and dream of the soft look
Your eyes had once, and of their shadows deep;

How many loved your moments of glad grace,
And loved your beauty with love false or true,
But one man loved the pilgrim soul in you,
And loved the sorrows of your changing face;

And bending down beside the glowing bars,
Murmur, a little sadly, how Love fled
And paced upon the mountains overhead,
And hid his face amid a crowd of stars.

W. B. Yeats

THAT THE NIGHT COME

She lived in storm and strife,
Her soul had such desire
For what proud death may bring
That it could not endure
The common good of life,
But lived as 'twere a king
That packed his marriage day
With banneret and pennon,
Trumpet and kettledrum,
And the outrageous cannon,
To bundle time away
That the night come.

W. B. Yeats

DEATH

Nor dread nor hope attend
A dying animal;
A man awaits his end
Dreading and hoping all;
Many times he died,
Many times rose again.
A great man in his pride
Confronting murderous men
Casts derision upon
Supersession of breath;
He knows death to the bone—
Man has created death.

W. B. Yeats

THE DEATH AND LAST CONFESSION
OF WANDERING PETER

When Peter Wanderwide was young
He wandered everywhere he would:
And all that he approved was sung,
And most of what he saw was good.

When Peter Wanderwide was thrown
By Death himself beyond Auxerre,
He chanted in heroic tone
To priests and people gathered there:

"If all that I have loved and seen
Be with me on the Judgment Day,
I shall be saved the crowd between
From Satan and his foul array.

"Almighty God will surely cry,
'St. Michael! Who is this that stands
With Ireland in his dubious eye,
And Perigord between his hands,

"'And on his arm the stirrup-thongs,
And in his gait the narrow seas,
And in his mouth Burgundian songs,
But in his heart the Pyrenees?'

"St. Michael then will answer right
(And not without angelic shame),
'I seem to know his face by sight:
I cannot recollect his name . . .?'

"St. Peter will befriend me then,
Because my name is Peter too:
'I know him for the best of men
That ever wallopped barley brew.

"'And though I did not know him well
And though his soul were clogged with sin,
I hold the keys of Heaven and Hell.
Be welcome, noble Peterkin.'

"Then shall I spread my native wings
And tread secure the heavenly floor,
And tell the Blessed doubtful things
Of Val d'Aran and Perigord."

* * *

This was the last and solemn jest
Of weary Peter Wanderwide.
He spoke it with a failing zest,
And having spoken it, he died.

Hilaire Belloc

AUVERGNAT

There was a man was half a clown
(It's so my father tells of it).
He saw the church in Clermont town
And laughed to hear the bells of it.

He laughed to hear the bells that ring
In Clermont Church and round of it;
He heard the verger's daughter sing,
And loved her for the sound of it.

The verger's daughter said him nay;
She had the right of choice in it.
He left the town at break of day:
He hadn't had a voice in it.

The road went up, the road went down,
And there the matter ended it.
He broke his heart in Clermont town,
At Pontgibaud they mended it.

Hilaire Belloc

HOW DID THE PARTY GO?

How did the party go in Portman Square?
    I cannot tell you; Juliet was not there.
And how did Lady Gaster's party go?
    Juliet was next me, and I do not know.

Hilaire Belloc

THE LIKENESS

When I came forth this morn I saw
Quite twenty cloudlets in the air;
And then I saw a flock of sheep,
Which told me how those clouds came there.

That flock of sheep, on that green grass,
Well might it lie so still and proud!
Its likeness had been drawn in heaven
On a blue sky, in silvery cloud.

I gazed me up, I gazed me down,
And swore, though good the likeness was,
'Twas a long way from justice done
To such white wool, such sparkling grass.

W. H. Davies

A GREAT TIME

Sweet Chance, that led my steps abroad,
Beyond the town, where wild flowers grow—
A rainbow and a cuckoo, Lord,
How rich and great the times are now!
Know, all ye sheep
And cows, that keep
On staring that I stand so long
In grass that's wet from heavy rain—
A rainbow and a cuckoo's song
May never come together again;
May never come
This side the tomb.

W. H. Davies

THE DONKEY

When fishes flew and forests walked,
And figs grew upon thorn,
Some moment when the moon was blood,
Then surely I was born;

With monstrous head and sickening cry
And ears like errant wings,
The devil's walking parody
On all four-footed things.

The tattered outlaw of the earth,
Of ancient crooked will;
Starve, scourge, deride me: I am dumb,
I keep my secret still.

Fools! For I also had my hour;
One far fierce hour and sweet:
There was a shout about my ears,
And palms before my feet.

G. K. Chesterton

THE PRAISE OF DUST

"What of vile dust?" the preacher said.
Methought the whole world woke,
The dead stone lived beneath my foot,
And my whole body spoke.

"You, that play tyrant to the dust,
And stamp its wrinkled face,
This patient star that flings you not
Far into homeless space,

"Come down out of your dusty shrine
The living dust to see,
The flowers that at your sermon's end
Stand blazing silently.

"Rich white and blood-red blossom; stones,
Lichens like fire encrust;
A gleam of blue, a glare of gold,
The vision of the dust.

"Pass them all by: till, as you come
Where, at a city's edge,
Under a tree—I know it well—
Under a lattice ledge,

"The sunshine falls on one brown head.
You, too, O cold of clay,
Eater of stones, may haply hear
The trumpets of that day

"When God to all his paladins
By his own splendour swore
To make a fairer face than heaven
Of dust and nothing more."

G. K. Chesterton

BLONDIE GOES TO HEAVEN

Paul said and Peter said
And all the saints alive or dead
Vowed she had the sweetest head
Of yellow, yellow hair.

Anonymous

THE BELLS OF HEAVEN

'Twould ring the bells of Heaven
The wildest peal for years,
If Parson lost his senses
And people came to theirs,
And he and they together
Knelt down with angry prayers
For tamed and shabby tigers
And dancing dogs and bears,
And wretched, blind pit ponies,
And little hunted hares.

Ralph Hodgson

TIME, YOU OLD
GIPSY MAN

Time, you old gipsy man,
Will you not stay,
Put up your caravan
Just for one day?

All things I'll give you
Will you be my guest,
Bells for your jennet
Of silver the best,
Goldsmiths shall beat you
A great golden ring,
Peacocks shall bow to you,
Little boys sing,
Oh, and sweet girls will
Festoon you with may,
Time, you old gipsy,
Why hasten away?

Last week in Babylon,
Last night in Rome,
Morning, and in the crush
Under Paul's dome;
Under Paul's dial
You tighten your rein—
Only a moment,
And off once again;
Off to some city
Now blind in the womb,
Off to another
Ere that's in the tomb.

Time, you old gipsy man,
Will you not stay,
Put up your caravan
Just for one day?

Ralph Hodgson

From THE SONG OF HONOUR

I climbed a hill as light fell short,
And rooks came home in scramble sort,
And filled the trees and flapped and fought
And sang themselves to sleep;
An owl from nowhere with no sound
Swung by and soon was nowhere found,
I heard him calling half-way round,
Holloing loud and deep;
A pair of stars, faint pins of light,
Then many a star, sailed into sight,
And all the stars, the flower of night.
Were round me at a leap;

To tell how still the valleys lay
I heard a watchdog miles away,
And bells of distant sheep.
It seemed, so still the valleys were,
As if the whole world knelt at prayer,
Save me and me alone;
So pure and wide that silence was
I feared to bend a blade of grass,
And there I stood like stone.

There sharp and sudden, there I heard—
   Ah! some wild lovesick singing bird
   Woke singing in the trees?
   The nightingale and babble-wren
   Were in the English greenwood then,
   And you heard one of these?
The babble-wren and nightingale
Sang in the Abyssinian vale
That season of the year!
Yet, true enough, I heard them plain,
I heard them both again, again,
As sharp and sweet and clear
As if the Abyssinian tree
Had thrust a bough across the sea,
Had thrust a bough across to me
With music for my ear!

I heard them both, and oh! I heard
The song of every singing bird
That sings beneath the sky,
And with the song of lark and wren
The song of mountains, moths and men
And seas and rainbows vie!

The song of men divinely wise
Who look and see in starry skies
Not stars so much as robins' eyes,
And when these pale away
Hear flocks of shiny pleiades
Among the plums and apple trees
Sing in the summer day—

The song of all both high and low
To some blest vision true,
The song of beggars when they throw
The crust of pity all men owe
To hungry sparrows in the snow,
Old beggars hungry too—
The song of kings of kingdoms when
They rise above their fortune, Men—
And crown themselves anew.

And song—that song whose singers come
With old kind tales of pity from
The Great Compassion's lips,
That make the bells of Heaven to peal
Round pillows frosty with the feel
Of Death's cold finger tips—

The song of men all sorts and kinds,
As many tempers, moods and minds
As leaves are on a tree,
As many faiths and castes and creeds,
As many human bloods and breeds
As in the world may be.

The music of a lion strong
That shakes a hill a whole night long,
A hill as loud as he,
The twitter of a mouse among
Melodious greenery,
The ruby's and the rainbow's song,
The nightingale's—all three,
The song of life that wells and flows
From every leopard, lark and rose
And everything that gleams or goes
Lack-lustre in the sea.

I heard it all, I heard the whole
Harmonious hymn of being roll
Up through the chapel of my soul
And at the altar die,
And in the awful quiet then
Myself I heard, Amen, Amen,
Amen I heard me cry!
I heard it all and then although
I caught my flying senses, Oh,
A dizzy man was I!
I stood and stared; the sky was lit,
The sky was stars all over it,
I stood, I knew not why,
Without a wish, without a will,
I stood upon that silent hill
And stared into the sky until
My eyes were blind with stars and still
I stared into the sky.

Ralph Hodgson

THE FLY

How large unto the tiny fly
Must little things appear!—
A rosebud like a feather-bed,
Its prickle like a spear;

A dewdrop like a looking-glass
A hair like golden wire;
The smallest grain of mustard-seed
As fierce as coals of fire;

A loaf of bread, a lofty hill;
A wasp, a cruel leopard;
And specks of salt as bright to see
As lambkins to a shepherd.

Walter de la Mare

THE LISTENERS

"Is there anybody there?" said the Traveller,
Knocking on the moonlit door;
And his horse in the silence champed the grasses
Of the forest's ferny floor:
And a bird flew up out of the turret,
Above the Traveller's head:
And he smote upon the door again a second time;
"Is there anybody there?" he said.
But no one descended to the Traveller;
No head from the leaf-fringed sill
Leaned over and looked into his gray eyes,
Where he stood perplexed and still.
But only a host of phantom listeners
That dwelt in the lone house then
Stood listening in the quiet of the moonlight
To that voice from the world of men:

Stood thronging the faint moonbeams on the dark
    stair,
That goes down to the empty hall,
Hearkening in an air stirred and shaken
By the lonely Traveller's call.
And he felt in his heart their strangeness,
Their stillness answering his cry,
While his horse moved, cropping the dark turf,
'Neath the starred and leafy sky;
For he suddenly smote on the door, even
Louder, and lifted his head:—
"Tell them I came, and no one answered,
That I kept my word," he said.
Never the least stir made the listeners,
Though every word he spake
Fell echoing through the shadowiness of the still
    house
From the one man left awake:
Ay, they heard his foot upon the stirrup,
And the sound of iron on stone,
And how the silence surged softly backward
When the plunging hoofs were gone.

Walter de la Mare

A FARMER'S BOY

They strolled down the lane together,
The sky was studded with stars.
They reached the gate in silence,
And he lifted down the bars.
She neither smiled nor thanked him
Because she knew not how;
For he was just a farmer's boy
And she a Jersey cow . . .   **Anonymous**

THE PASTURE

I'm going out to clean the pasture spring;
I'll only stop to rake the leaves away
(And wait to watch the water clear, I may):
I sha'n't be gone long.—You come too.

I'm going out to fetch the little calf
That's standing by the mother. It's so young
It totters when she licks it with her tongue.
I sha'n't be gone long.—You come too.

Robert Frost

ACQUAINTED WITH THE NIGHT

I have been one acquainted with the night.
I have walked out in rain—and back in rain.
I have outwalked the furthest city light.

I have looked down the saddest city lane.
I have passed by the watchman on his beat
And dropped my eyes, unwilling to explain.

I have stood still and stopped the sound of feet
When far away an interrupted cry
Came over houses from another street,

But not to call me back or say good-bye;
And further still at an unearthly height,
One luminary clock against the sky

Proclaimed the time was neither wrong nor right.
I have been one acquainted with the night.

Robert Frost

COME IN

As I came to the edge of the woods,
Thrush music—hark!
Now if it was dusk outside,
Inside it was dark.

Too dark in the woods for a bird
By sleight of wing
To better its perch for the night,
Though it still could sing.

The last of the light of the sun
That had died in the west
Still lived for one song more
In a thrush's breast.

Far in the pillared dark
Thrush music went—
Almost like a call to come in
To the dark and lament.

But no, I was out for stars:
I would not come in.
I meant not even if asked,
And I hadn't been.

Robert Frost

THE MORON

See the happy moron,
He doesn't give a damn!
I wish I were a moron—
My God! Perhaps I am!

Anonymous

OUR STORY

There was a young king who was sad,
And a young queen who was lonely;
They lived together their busy life,
Known to each other only,—

Known to each other with strange love,
But with sighs for the king's vain sorrow
And for the queen's vain loneliness
And vain forethought of the morrow.

After a barren while they died,
In death they were not parted:
Now in their grave perhaps they know
Why they were broken-hearted.

Thomas MacDonagh

NOAH AND THE RABBIT

"No land," said Noah,
"There-is-not-any-land.
Oh, Rabbit, Rabbit, can't you understand?"

But Rabbit shook his head:
"Say it again," he said;
"And slowly, please.
No good brown earth for burrows,
And no trees;
No wastes where vetch and rabbit-parsley grows,
No brakes, no bushes and no turnip rows,
No holt, no upland, meadowland or weald,
No tangled hedgerow and no playtime field?"

"No land at all—just water," Noah replied,

And Rabbit sighed.
"For always, Noah?" he whispered, "will there be
Nothing henceforth for ever but the sea?
Or will there come a day
When the green earth will call me back to play?"

Noah bowed his head:
"Some day . . . some day," he said.

Hugh Chesterman

THE WEST WIND

It's a warm wind, the west wind, full of birds' cries;
I never hear the west wind but tears are in my eyes.
For it comes from the west lands, the old brown hills,
And April's in the west wind, and daffodils.

It's a fine land, the west land, for hearts as tired as
    mine,
Apple orchards blossom there, and the air's like
    wine.
There is cool green grass there, where men may lie
    at rest,
And the thrushes are in song there, fluting from the
    nest.

"Will ye not come home, brother? ye have been
    long away,
It's April, and blossom time, and white is the may:
And bright is the sun, brother, and warm is the
    rain,—
Will ye not come home, brother, home to us again?

"The young corn is green, brother, where the rabbits
    run,
It's blue sky, and white clouds, and warm rain and
    sun.
It's song to a man's soul, brother, fire to a man's
    brain,
 To hear the wild bees and see the merry spring
    again.

"Larks are singing in the west, brother, above the
    green wheat,
So will ye not come home, brother, and rest your
    tired feet?
I've a balm for bruised hearts, brother, sleep for
    aching eyes,"
Says the warm wind, the west wind, full of birds'
    cries.

It's the white road westwards is the road I must
    tread
To the green grass, the cool grass, and rest for heart
    and head,
To the violets and the warm hearts and the thrushes'
    song,
In the fine land, the west land, the land where I
    belong.

John Masefield

I COULD NOT SLEEP FOR THINKING
OF THE SKY

I could not sleep for thinking of the sky,
The unending sky, with all its million suns
Which turn their planets everlastingly
In nothing, where the fire-haired comet runs.
If I could sail that nothing, I should cross
Silence and emptiness with dark stars passing;
Then, in the darkness, see a point of gloss
Burn to a glow, and glare, and keep amassing,
And rage into a sun with wandering planets,
And drop behind; and then, as I proceed,
See his last light upon his last moon's granites
Die to a dark that would be night indeed:
Night where my soul might sail a million years
In nothing, not even Death, not even tears.

John Masefield

WILL YOU COME?

Will you come?
Will you come?
Will you ride
So late
At my side?
O, will you come?

Will you come?
Will you come
If the night
Has a moon,
Full and bright?
O, will you come?

Would you come?
Would you come
If the noon
Gave light,
Not the moon?
Beautiful, would you come?

Would you have come?
Would you have come
Without scorning,
Had it been
Still morning?
Belovèd, would you have come?

If you come
Haste and come.
Owls have cried;
It grows dark
To ride.
Belovèd, beautiful, come.

Edward Thomas

THE OWL

Downhill I came, hungry, and yet not starved;
Cold, yet had heat within me that was proof
Against the North wind; tired, yet so that rest
Had seemed the sweetest thing under a roof.

Then at the inn I had food, fire, and rest,
Knowing how hungry, cold, and tired was I.
All of the night was quite barred out except
An owl's cry, a most melancholy cry

Shaken out long and clear upon the hill,
No merry note, nor cause of merriment,
But one telling me plain what I escaped
And others could not, that night, as in I went.

And salted was my food, and my repose,
Salted and sobered, too, by the bird's voice
Speaking for all who lay under the stars,
Soldiers and poor, unable to rejoice.

Edward Thomas

THE CONSCIENTIOUS DEACON

Black cats, grey cats, green cats miau—
Chasing the deacon who stole the cow.

He runs and tumbles, he tumbles and runs.
He sees big white men with dogs and guns.

He falls down flat. He turns to stare—
No cats, no dogs, and no men there.

But black shadows, grey shadows, green shadows
    come.
The wind says, "Miau!" and the rain says, "Hum!"

He goes straight home. He dreams all night.
He howls. He puts his wife in a fright.

Black devils, grey devils, green devils shine—
Yes, by Sambo,
And the fire looks fine!

16—B.H.

Cat devils, dog devils, cow devils grin—
Yes, by Sambo,
And the fire rolls in.

And so, next day, to avoid the worst—
He takes that cow
Where he found her first.

Vachel Lindsay

THE LEADEN-EYED

Let not young souls be smothered out before
They do quaint deeds and fully flaunt their pride.
It is the world's one crime its babes grow dull,
Its poor are ox-like, limp and leaden-eyed.
Not that they starve, but starve so dreamlessly;
Not that they sow, but that they seldom reap;
Not that they serve, but have no gods to serve;
Not that they die, but that they die like sheep.

Vachel Lindsay

MILK FOR THE CAT

When the tea is brought at five o'clock,
And all the neat curtains are drawn with care,
The little black cat with bright green eyes
Is suddenly purring there.

At first she pretends, having nothing to do,
She has come in merely to blink by the grate,
But, though tea may be late or the milk may be sour,
She is never late.

And presently her agate eyes
Take a soft large, milky haze
And her independent casual glance
Becomes a stiff, hard gaze.

Then she stamps her claws or lifts her ears,
Or twists her tail and begins to stir,
Till suddenly all her lithe body becomes
One breathing, trembling purr.

The children eat and wriggle and laugh,
The two old ladies stroke their silk:
But the cat is grown small and thin with desire,
Transformed to a creeping lust for milk.

The white saucer like some full moon descends
At last from the clouds of the table above;
She sighs and dreams and thrills and glows,
Transfigured with love.

She nestles over the shining rim,
Buries her chin in the creamy sea;
Her tail hangs loose; each drowsy paw
Is doubled under each bending knee.

A long, dim ecstasy holds her life;
Her world is an infinite shapeless white,
Till her tongue has curled the last holy drop,
Then she sinks back into the night,

Draws and dips her body to heap
Her sleepy nerves in the great arm-chair,
Lies defeated and buried deep
Three or four hours unconscious there.

Harold Monro

WEEK-END

The train! The twelve o'clock for paradise.
Hurry, or it will try to creep away.
Out in the country everyone is wise:
We can be only wise on Saturday.
There you are waiting, little friendly house:
Those are your chimney-stacks with you between,
Surrounded by old trees and strolling cows,
Staring through all your windows at the green.
Your homely floor is creaking for our tread;
The smiling tea-pot with contented spout
Thinks of the boiling water, and the bread
Longs for the butter. All their hands are out
To greet us, and the gentle blankets seem
Purring and crooning: "Lie in us, and dream".

Harold Monro

CATS AND KINGS

With wide unblinking stare
The cat looked; but she did not see the king.
She only saw a two-legged creature there
Who, in due time, might have tit-bits to fling.

The king was on his throne.
In his left hand he grasped the golden ball.
She looked at him with eyes of bright green stone,
And thought, *What fun if he should let it fall.*

With swishing tail she lay
And watched for happy accidents, while he,
The essential king, was brooding far away
In his own world with hope and memory.

O, cats are subtle now,
And kings are mice to many a modern mind;
And yet there throbbed behind that human brow
The strangely simple thoughts that serve mankind.

The gulf might not be wide;
But over it, at least, no cat could spring.
So once again an ancient adage lied.
The cat looked; but she never saw the king.

Alfred Noyes

ST VALENTINE'S WAY

"Good morrow, gallant Lover!"
　　"Good morrow, saintly Sir!"
"I've just seen your Sweetheart."
　　"And how did you know her?"
"How could I help but know her?
She was swift to recognise,
For her face was like a rose,
And like violets her eyes;
Herself was sweet as sugar,
As any man could see—
Now was not this your Sweetheart?"
　　"In truth, sir, this was she."

"Good morrow, pretty Sweetheart."
　　"Good morrow, gentle Saint."
"I've just come from your Lover."
　　"And how were you acquaint?"
"I could pick him from a thousand
In the middle of the night,
For his eye was like an eagle's,
And his arm was full of might;

He was the comeliest man alive,
As any girl could see—
Now was not this your Lover?"
    "Indeed, sir, this was he."

So says the young Saint Valentine
To-day where'er he goes
To all the lads and lasses—
And they wonder how he knows.

Eleanor Farjeon

THE CAROL SINGERS

They come in ones and twos and threes,
Small ragged girls and boys,
Whose homes will show no Christmas-trees,
Whose stockings hold no toys;
And shuffling on the step at night,
They—sing? Well, to be kind, not quite—
They make a sort of noise.

Not in the hope of myrrh and gold
And frankincense they sing,
As they a hackneyed verse unfold
About a new-born King.
They rate their gabbled effort at
A penny, and it's scarce worth that
When they go carolling.

A try-on? Yes. But as for me
I never can refuse
The rough unpractised minstrelsy
That tells of heavenly news.
A child once in a stable lay—
How can I empty send away
These children from the Mews?

Eleanor Farjeon

THE WOOD OF FLOWERS

I went to the Wood of Flowers,
No one went with me;
I was there alone for hours;
I was happy as could be,
In the Wood of Flowers!

There was grass
On the ground;
There were leaves
On the tree;

And the wind
Had a sound
Of such sheer
Gaiety,

That I
Was as happy
As happy could be,
In the Wood of Flowers!

James Stephens

WHAT TOMAS SAID IN A PUB

I saw God! Do you doubt it?
Do you dare to doubt it?
I saw the Almighty Man! His hand
Was resting on a mountain! And
He looked upon the World, and all about it:
I saw Him plainer than you see me now
—You mustn't doubt it!

He was not satisfied!
His look was all dissatisfied!
His beard swung on a wind, far out of sight
Behind the world's curve! And there was light
Most fearful from His forehead! And He sighed:
—That star went always wrong, and from the start
I was dissatisfied!—

He lifted up His hand!
I say He heaved a dreadful hand
Over the spinning earth! Then I said,—Stay,
You must not strike it, God! I'm in the way!
And I will never move from where I stand!—
He said,—Dear child, I feared that you were dead,—
... And stayed His hand!

James Stephens

LITTLE THINGS

Little things, that run, and quail,
And die, in silence and despair!

Little things, that fight, and fail,
And fall, on sea, and earth, and air!

All trapped and frightened little things,
The mouse, the coney, hear our prayer!

As we forgive those done to us,
—The lamb, the linnet, and the hare—

Forgive us all our trespasses,
Little creatures, everywhere!

James Stephens

THE FULNESS OF TIME

On a rusty iron throne,
Past the furthest star of space,
I saw Satan sit alone,
Old and haggard was his face;
For his work was done, and he
Rested in eternity.

And to him from out the sun
Came his father and his friend,
Saying,—Now thy work is done
Enmity is at an end;
And He guided Satan to
Paradises that He knew.

Gabriel, without a frown;
Uriel, without a spear;
Raphael, came winging down,
Welcoming their ancient peer;
And they seated him beside
One who had been crucified.

James Stephens

IN THE COOL OF THE EVENING

I thought I heard Him calling! Did you hear
A sound? a little sound!
My curious ear
Is dinned with flying noises; and the tree
Goes—whisper, whisper, whisper, silently,
Till all its whispers spread into the sound
Of a dull roar. . . .

—Lie closer to the ground:
The shade is deep, and He may pass us by,
We are so very small, and His great eye,
Customed to starry majesties, may gaze
Too wide to spy us hiding in the maze.

—Ah, misery! The sun has not yet gone,
And we are naked! He will look upon
Our crouching shame! May make us stand upright,
Burning in terror—O that it were night—!
He may not come . . . What? Listen! Listen now—
He's here! Lie closer . . . *Adam, where art thou?*

James Stephens

TO A POET A THOUSAND
YEARS HENCE

I who am dead a thousand years,
And wrote this sweet archaic song,
Send you my words for messengers
The way I shall not pass along.

I care not if you bridge the seas,
Or ride secure the cruel sky,
Or build consummate palaces
Of metal or of masonry.

But have you wine and music still,
And statues and a bright-eyed love,
And foolish thoughts of good or ill,
And prayers to them who sit above?

How shall we conquer? Like a wind
That falls at eve our fancies blow,
And old Mæonides the blind
Said it three thousand years ago.

O friend unseen, unborn, unknown,
Student of our sweet English tongue,
Read out my words at night, alone:
I was a poet, I was young.

Since I can never see your face,
And never shake you by the hand,
I send my soul through time and space
To greet you. You will understand.

James Elroy Flecker

PUT UP AGAIN THY SWORD INTO ITS PLACE

"Put up thy sword." So Peter found
Rebuke upon his weapon's aid,
The High Priest's servant of his wound
Was healed, and the disciple's blade
Re-bidden to its scabbard. See,
O World, the lovely evidence—
True lesson of Gethsemane—
That Heaven on Earth disdains defence.
For still the hostile ages pass,
And force may strive for right, but know,
You cannot cut at Caiaphas
But the hired servant bears the blow;
And still the apostle, he who dies
In thought to stem Christ's Passion, falls
Short of his fervour and denies
His Master in the High Priest's halls . . .

Forth leaps the sword upon the same
Innocent pretexts—little homes,
Childhood and womanhood wronged, the Name
Of this rebuking Christ: hence comes
A votive fury that begins
All conflicts; and the justest pride
Is first the stalking-horse of sins
And then deserted and denied.
Despots, diplomatists, dark trades
Set men unceasingly at strife,
Usurp the war-cries of crusades,
Divert each God-devoted life;
Never, O never yet, will war,
How-e'er so poisonous root and stem,
Lack the assurance of a star
Out-dazzling His of Bethlehem
Till Truth and Innocence reprove
Their ghastly champions with His word—
Who chid the violence even of love—
"Put up thy sword."   Put up thy sword!

Helen Parry Eden

MAY DAY

A delicate fabric of bird-song
Floats in the air,
The smell of wet wild earth
Is everywhere.

Red small leaves of the maple
Are clenched like a hand,
Like girls at their first communion
The pear trees stand.

Oh I must pass nothing by
Without loving it much:
The raindrop try with my lips,
The grass with my touch;

For how can I be sure
I shall see again
The world on the first of May
Shining after the rain?

Sara Teasdale

THERE IS A TIME

No doubt a sonnet, even in modern style,
Would have to rhyme, but need it have a lilt?
If a modern block of offices can be built,
Plain, blank, bleak as a cabinet file—
Forswearing all temptations to beguile
Our sense with any curve, recess, or tilt—
Yet serve its business purpose to the hilt,
May not a verse speak Love without a smile?
Perhaps: but note that poets on this excursion
Seeking escape from well-worn metric norms,
Take to the biblical lilt of the Authorised Version . . .
There is a time for stern rhetorical forms. . . .
There is a time to trot; and a time to prance;
A time to creep; and a time, O Love, to dance!

Frederic J. Osborn

ENVOI

Go, dumb-born book,
Tell her that sang me once that song of Lawes:
Hadst thou but song
As thou hast subjects known,
Then were there cause in thee that should condone
Even my faults that heavy upon me lie,
And build her glories their longevity.

Tell her that sheds
Such treasure in the air,
Recking naught else but that her graces give
Life to the moment,
I would bid them live
As roses might, in magic amber laid,
Red overwrought with orange and all made
One substance and one colour
Braving time.

Tell her that goes
With song upon her lips
But sings not out the song, nor knows
The maker of it, some other mouth
May be as fair as hers,
Might, in new ages, gain her worshippers,
When our two dusts with Waller's shall be laid,
Siftings on siftings in oblivion,
Till change hath broken down
All things save Beauty alone.

Ezra Pound

Compare with Edmund Waller's "Go, Lovely Rose", page 71.

THE STARS

The stars rushed forth to-night
Fast on the faltering light;
So thick those stars did lie
No room was left for sky;
And to my upturned stare
A snow-storm filled the air.

Stars lay like yellow pollen
That from a flower has fallen;
And single stars I saw
Crossing themselves in awe;
Some stars in sudden fear
Fell like a falling tear.

What is the eye of man,
This little star that can
See all those stars at once,
Multitudinous suns,
Making of them a wind
That blows across the mind?

If eye can nothing see
But what is part of me,
I ask and ask again
With a persuasive pain,
What thing, O God, am I,
This mote and mystery?

Andrew Young

THE FARMER'S GUN

The wood is full of rooks
That by their faded looks
No more on thievery will thrive,
As when they were alive,
Nor fill the air with the hoarse noise
That most of all is England's pleasant voice.

How ugly is this work of man,
Seen in the bald brain-pan,
Voracious bill,
Torn wing, uprooted quill
And host of tiny glistening flies
That lend false lustre to these empty eyes.

More delicate is nature's way
Whereby all creatures know their day,
And hearing Death call "Come,
Here is a bone or crumb",
Bury themselves before they die
And leave no trace of foul mortality.

Andrew Young

THE SLOW RACE

I followed each detour
Of the slow meadow-winding Stour,
That looked on cloud, tree, hill,
And mostly flowed by standing still.

Fearing to go too quick
I stopped at times to throw a stick
Or see how in the copse
The last snow was the first snowdrops.

The river also tarried
So much of sky and earth it carried,
Or even changed its mind
To flow back with a flaw of wind.

And when we reached the weir
That combed the water's silver hair,
I knew I lost the race—
I could not keep so slow a pace.

Andrew Young

THE OLD NURSE

I cannot but believe, though you were dead,
Lying stone-still, and I came in and said
Having been out perhaps in mud and rain:
"O dear, O look, I have torn my skirt again,"
That you would rise with the old simple ease,
And say, "Yes, child," and come to me. And there
In your white crackling apron, on your knees
With your quick hands, rough with the washing-up
Of every silver spoon and cherished cup,
And bending head, coiled with the happy hair
Your own child should have pulled for you (but no,
Your child who might have been, you did not bear,
Because the endless riches of your care
Were all for us) you would mend and heal my tear—
Mend, touch and heal; and stitching all the while,
Your cottons on the floor, look up and show
The sudden light perpetual of your smile—
Then, with your darning finished, being dead
Go back and lie, like stone, upon your bed.

Frances Cornford

17—B.H.

THE COUNTRY BEDROOM

My room's a square and candle-lighted boat,
In the surrounding depths of night afloat;
My windows are the portholes, and the seas
The sound of rain on the dark apple-trees.

Seamonster-like beneath, an old horse blows
A snort of darkness from his sleeping nose,
Below, among drowned daisies. Far off, hark!
Far off one owl amidst the waves of dark.

Frances Cornford

THE WHALE AND JONAH

He sported round the watery world.
His rich oil was a gloomy waveless lake
Within the waves. Affrighted seamen hurled
Their weapons in his foaming wake.

One old corroding iron he bore
Which journeyed through his flesh but yet had not
Found out his life. Another lance he wore
Outside him, pricking in a tender spot.

So distant were his parts that they
Sent but a dull faint message to his brain.
He knew not his own flesh, as great kings may
Not know the farther places where they reign.

His play made storm in a calm sea;
His very kindness killed what he might touch;
And wrecks lay scattered on his anger's lee.
The Moon rocked to and fro his watery couch.

His hunger cleared the sea. And where
He passed, the ocean's edge lifted its brim.
He skimmed the dim sea-floor to find if there
Some garden had its harvest ripe for him.

But in his sluggish brain no thought
Ever arose. His law was instinct blind.
No thought or gleam or vision ever brought
Light to the dark of his old dreamless mind.

Until one day, sudden and strange,
Half-hints of knowledge burst upon his sight.
Glimpses he had of Time, and Space, and Change,
And something greater than his might;

And terror's leap to imagine sin;
And blinding Truth half-bare unto his seeing.
It was the living man who had come in . . .
Jonah's thoughts flying through his being.

Viola Meynell

THE BLIND MAN'S
MORNING

Sleeping, he is not blind
More than another.
But dawn's faint wind,
Blowing rosy light,
Whispers: Rise, brother,
To thy night.

Viola Meynell

THE OLD HORSE IN THE FIELD

White on his back remains the snow;
He stands but a few paces changed
From where he stood some hours ago;
Snow clouds, cold hills, are round him ranged;
A frozen bird lies by the hedge.
And, as he stands, his scanty blood,
Like the thin stream at the field's edge,
Slackens the flow of its faint cold flood.
"O sun," I prayed as I went past,
"If that great day of life draws near
When you shall bless the world at last,
Let your first beam fall here."

Viola Meynell

ONLY OF YOU AND ME

Only of you and me the night wind sings,
Only of us the sailors speak at sea,
The earth is filled with wondered whisperings
Only of you and me.

Only of you and me the breakers chant,
Only of us the stir in bush and tree;
The rain and sunshine tell the eager plant
Only of you and me.

Only of you and me, till all shall fade;
Only of us the whole world's thoughts can be—
For we are Love, and God himself is made
Only of you and me.

Louis Untermeyer

BASE DETAILS

If I were fierce, and bald, and short of breath,
I'd live with scarlet Majors at the Base,
And speed glum heroes up the line to death.
You'd see me with my puffy petulant face,
Guzzling and gulping in the best hotel,
Reading the Roll of Honour. "Poor young chap,"
I'd say—"I used to know his father well;
Yes, we've lost heavily in this last scrap."
And when the war is done and youth stone dead,
I'd toddle safely home and die—in bed.

Siegfried Sassoon

A PRAYER TO TIME

Time, that anticipates eternities
And has an art to resurrect the rose;
Time, whose lost siren song at evening blows
With sun-flushed cloud shoreward on toppling seas;
Time, arched by planets lonely in the vast
Sadness that darkens with the fall of day;
Time, unexplored elysium; and the grey
Death-shadow'd pyramid that we name the past—
Magnanimous Time, patient with man's vain glory;
Ambition's road; Lethe's awaited guest;
Time, hearkener to the stumbling passionate story
Of human failure humanly confessed;
Time, on whose stair we dream our hopes of heaven,
Help us to judge ourselves, and so be shriven.

Siegfried Sassoon

TO AN OLD LADY DEAD

Old lady, when last year I sipped your tea
And wooed you with my deference to discuss
The elegance of your embroidery,
I felt no forethought of our meeting thus.
Last week your age was "almost eighty-three."
To-day you own the eternal over-plus.
These moments are "experience" for me;
But not for you; not for a mutual "us."

I visit you unwelcomed; you've no time
Left to employ in afternoon politeness.
You've only Heaven's great stairway now to climb,
And your long load of years has changed to lightness.
When Oxford belfries chime you do not hear,
Nor in this mellow-toned autumnal brightness
Observe an English-School-like atmosphere . . .
You have inherited everlasting whiteness.

You lived your life in grove and garden shady
Of social Academe, good talk and taste:
But now you are a very quiet old lady,
Stiff, sacrosanct, and alabaster-faced.
And, while I tip-toe awe-struck from your room,
I fail to synthesize your earth-success
With this, your semblance to a sculptured tomb
That clasps a rosary of nothingness.

Siegfried Sassoon

THE BUSY HEART

Now that we've done our best and worst, and
   parted,
I would fill my mind with thoughts that will not
   rend.
(O heart, I do not dare go empty-hearted)
I'll think of Love in books, Love without end;
Women with child, content; and old men sleeping;
And wet strong ploughlands, scarred for certain
   grain;
And babes that weep, and so forget their weeping;
And the young heavens, forgetful after rain;
And evening hush, broken by homing wings;
And Song's nobility, and Wisdom holy,
That live, we dead. I would think of a thousand
   things,
Lovely and durable, and taste them slowly,
One after one, like tasting a sweet food.
I have need to busy my heart with quietude.

Rupert Brooke

HEAVEN

Fish (fly-replete, in depth of June
Dawdling away their wat'ry noon)
Ponder deep wisdom, dark or clear,
Each secret fishy hope or fear.
Fish say, they have their Stream and Pond
But is there anything Beyond?
This life cannot be All, they swear,
For how unpleasant, if it were!
One may not doubt that, somehow, good
Shall come of Water and of Mud;

And, sure, the reverent eye must see
A Purpose in Liquidity.
We darkly know, by Faith we cry,
The future is not Wholly Dry.
Mud unto Mud!—Death eddies near—
Not here the appointed End, not here!
But somewhere, beyond Space and Time,
Is wetter water, slimier slime!
And there (they trust) there swimmeth One
Who swam ere rivers were begun,
Immense, of fishy form and mind,
Squamous, omnipotent, and kind;
And under that Almighty Fin
The littlest fish may enter in.
Oh! never fly conceals a hook,
Fish say, in the Eternal Brook,
But more than mundane weeds are there,
And mud, celestially fair;
Fat caterpillars drift around,
And Paradisal grubs are found;
Unfading moths, immortal flies,
And the worm that never dies.
And in that Heaven of all their wish,
There shall be no more land, say fish.

Rupert Brooke

THE RETURN

The veteran Greeks came home
Sleepwandering from the war.
We saw the galleys come
Blundering over the bar.
Each soldier with his scar
In rags and tatters came home.

Reading the wall of Troy
Ten years without a change
Was such intense employ
(Just out of the arrows' range),
All the world was strange
After ten years of Troy.

Their eyes knew every stone
In the huge heartbreaking wall
Year after year grown
Till there was nothing at all
But an alley steep and small,
Tramped earth and towering stone.

Now even the hills seemed low
In the boundless sea and land,
Weakened by distance so.
How could they understand
Space empty on every hand
And the hillocks squat and low?

And when they arrived at last
They found a childish scene
Embosomed in the past,
And the war lying between—
A child's preoccupied scene
When they came home at last.

But everything trite and strange,
The piece, the parcelled ground,
The vinerows—never a change!
The past and the present bound
In one oblivious round
Past thinking trite and strange.

But for their grey-haired wives
And their sons grown shy and tall
They would have given their lives
To raise the battered wall
Again, if this was all
In spite of their sons and wives.

Penelope in her tower
Looked down upon the show
And saw within an hour
Each man to his wife go,
Hesitant, sure and slow:
She, alone in her tower.

Edwin Muir

THE LITTLE GHOST WHO DIED FOR LOVE

Deborah Churchill, born 1678, was hanged 1708 for shielding her lover after a duel in which he killed his opponent and then fled to Holland. According to the law at the time she was hanged in his stead. It is recorded that: "Though she died at peace with God, this malefactor could never understand the justice of her sentence, to the last moment of her life."

"Fear not, O maidens, shivering
As bunches of the dew-drenched leaves
In the calm moonlight . . . it is the cold sends
   quivering
My voice, a little nightingale that grieves.

"Now Time beats not, and dead Love is forgotten . . .
The spirit too is dead and dank and rotten,

"And I forget the moment when I ran
Between my lover and the sworded man—

Blinded with terror lest I lose his heart.
The sworded man dropped, and I saw depart

"Love and my lover and my life . . . he fled
And I was strung and hung upon the tree.
It is so cold now that my heart is dead
And drops through time . . . night is too dark to see

"Him still . . . But it is spring; upon the fruit-boughs
    of your lips,
Young maids, the dew like India's splendour drips.
Pass by among the strawberry beds, and pluck the
    berries
Cooled by the silver moon; pluck boughs of cherries
That seem the lovely lucent coral bough
(From streams of starry milk those branches grow)
That Cassiopeia feeds with her faint light,
Like Ethiopia ever jewelled bright.

"Those lovely cherries do enclose
Deep in their hearts the silver snows,

"And the small budding flowers upon the trees
Are filled with sweetness like the bags of bees.

"Forget my fate . . . but I, a moonlight ghost,
Creep down the strawberry paths and seek the lost
World, the apothecary at the Fair.
I, Deborah, in my long cloak of brown
Like the small nightingale that dances down
The cherried boughs, creep to the doctor's bare
Booth . . . cold as ivy in the air,
And, where I stand, the brown and ragged light
Holds something still beyond, hid from my sight.

"Once, plumaged like the sea, his swanskin head
Had wintry white quills . . . 'Hearken to the Dead . . .
I was a nightingale, but now I croak
Like some dark harpy hidden in night's cloak,
Upon the walls; among the Dead, am quick.
Oh, give me medicine, for the world is sick;
Not medicines planet-spotted like fritillaries
For country sins and old stupidities,
Nor potions you may give a country maid
When she is lovesick . . . love in earth is laid,
Grown dead and rotten' . . . so I sank me down,
Poor Deborah in my long cloak of brown.

"Though cockcrow marches crying of false dawns
Shall bury my dark voice, yet still it mourns
Among the ruins,—for it is not I
But this old world, is sick and soon must die!"

Edith Sitwell

MACAVITY: THE MYSTERY CAT

Macavity's a Mystery Cat: he's called the Hidden
    Paw—
For he's the master criminal who can defy the Law.
He's the bafflement of Scotland Yard, the Flying
    Squad's despair:
For when they reach the scene of crime—*Macavity's
    not there!*

Macavity, Macavity, there's no one like Macavity,
He's broken every human law, he breaks the law of
    gravity.

His powers of levitation would make a fakir stare,
And when you reach the scene of crime—*Macavity's
not there!*
You may seek him in the basement, you may look
up in the air—
But I tell you once and once again, *Macavity's not
there!*

Macavity's a ginger cat, he's very tall and thin;
You would know him if you saw him, for his eyes
are sunken in.
His brow is deeply lined with thought, his head is
highly domed;
His coat is dusty from neglect, his whiskers are
uncombed.
He sways his head from side to side, with move-
ments like a snake;
And when you think he's half asleep, he's always
wide awake.

Macavity, Macavity, there's no one like Macavity,
For he's a fiend in feline shape, a monster of
depravity,
You may meet him in a by-street, you may see him
in the square—
But when a crime's discovered, then *Macavity's not
there!*

He's outwardly respectable (They say he cheats at
cards.)
And his footprints are not found in any file of Scotland Yard's.

And when the larder's looted, or the jewel-case is
    rifled,
Or when the milk is missing, or another Peke's been
    stifled,
Or the greenhouse glass is broken, and the trellis
    past repair—
Ay, there's the wonder of the thing! *Macavity's not
    there!*

And when the Foreign Office find a Treaty's gone
    astray,
Or the Admiralty lose some plans and drawings by
    the way,
There may be a scrap of paper in the hall or on the
    stair—
But it's useless to investigate—*Macavity's not there!*
And when the loss has been disclosed, the Secret
    Service say:
"It *must* have been Macavity!"—but he's a mile
    away.
You'll be sure to find him resting, or a-licking of his
    thumbs,
Or engaged in doing complicated long division sums.

Macavity, Macavity, there's no one like Macavity,
There never was a Cat of such deceitfulness and
    suavity.
He always has an alibi, and one or two to spare:
At whatever time the deed took place—MACAVITY
    WASN'T THERE!
And they say that all the Cats whose wicked deeds
    are widely known

(I might mention Mungojerrie, I might mention
   Griddlebone)
Are nothing more than agents for the Cat who all
   the time
Just controls their operations: the Napoleon of
   Crime!

T. S. Eliot

WHISPERS OF IMMORTALITY

Webster was much possessed by death
And saw the skull beneath the skin;
And breastless creatures under ground
Leaned backward with a lipless grin.

Daffodil bulbs instead of balls
Stared from the sockets of the eyes!
He knew that thought clings round dead limbs
Tightening its lusts and luxuries.

Donne, I suppose, was such another
Who found no substitute for sense,
To seize and clutch and penetrate;
Expert beyond experience,

He knew the anguish of the marrow
The ague of the skeleton;
No contact possible to flesh
Allayed the fever of the bone.

★ ★ ★

Grishkin is nice: her Russian eye
Is underlined for emphasis;
Uncorseted, her friendly bust
Gives promise of pneumatic bliss.

The couched Brazilian jaguar
Compels the scampering marmoset
With subtle effluence of cat;
Grishkin has a maisonette;

The sleek Brazilian jaguar
Does not in its arboreal gloom
Distil so rank a feline smell
As Grishkin in a drawing-room.

And even the Abstract Entities
Circumambulate her charm;
But our lot crawls between dry ribs
To keep our metaphysics warm.

T. S. Eliot

GOING TO SLEEP

I made the valley mine
With all its woods and streams,
I drew into myself the shine
Of the moon's white beams;
But though the valley and the heavenly steep
Came at my summons, yet I could not sleep.

I could not sleep until
I had renounced a part
Of my own self, too urgent will
And too possessive heart:
Oh with new love that scene and I were blessed
When each by each was equally possessed!

Then, then we slept. Wood, stream and I were
  gone,
And the white moon shared our oblivion.

George Rostrevor Hamilton

THE UNKNOWN TRAVELLER

You on the quay, or you who watch at the station,
Why do you wave—
You who never before
Met by field or shore—
Wave farewell to the unknown traveller faring?

You who mind the machine, or stoop to the harvest
Of shining grain,
Why do you break and rise,
The tears warm in your eyes,
To watch a flutter of smoke, a gay flag flying?

You shall forget, you never again shall see him,
Nor call to mind,
Whom now you greet and wave,
Ignorant, to his grave,
Over what orient lands, what undreamed oceans!

You, perchance, for a moment lost in travel
To the world's end,
Watching his banners pass,
Wave to yourself in the glass,
Wave farewell to the unknown traveller faring.

George Rostrevor Hamilton

From ROMANCE

When I was but thirteen or so
I went into a golden land,
Chimborazo, Cotopaxi
Took me by the hand.

My father died, my brother too,
They passed like fleeting dreams,
I stood where Popocatapetl
In the sunlight gleams.

I dimly heard the master's voice
And boys far-off at play,
Chimborazo, Cotopaxi
Had stolen me away.

I walked in a great golden dream
To and from my school—
Shining Popocatapetl
The dusty streets did rule.

I walked home with a gold dark boy
And never a word I'd say,
Chimborazo, Cotopaxi
Had taken my speech away.

The houses, people, traffic seemed
Thin fading dreams by day,
Chimborazo, Cotopaxi
They had stolen my soul away.

                                    W. J. Turner

TIME IS NOT MOCKED

Time is not mocked. Did you when you were five
Play ring-a-roses round the slow-foot second?
Go distant journeys twixt the tick and tock?
Perceive your mother, between beck and beckoned,
Age, sicken, die—and come again alive
(O wonderful!) with the rustle of her frock?
If I slipped sideways, breath-bound, swift and supple,
I could pass between the clock-beats to the closet
Not scraping either second of its bloom;
Then from their pegs, like clothes, new lives un-
    couple,
And try them on, 'gainst my own shape's deposit.
I was the He, the Hunter. Time was the stay-at-home.

My mother died when I was grown a man.
Eternity was ended. Time began.

Francis Meynell

IN PRAISE OF UNFAMOUS MEN

Time is our sculptor. He of earth and air,
Our mother's milk, our father's bone,
Quarries his stone.
What then?
Some he hews out in the huge shape of men
Heroic; some, more fair,
He with a subtler stroke
Graves as an imaged matrix in the rock:
The prophet and the poet and the seer,
Idol, idolator, iconoclast,
Mankind, man-mind, his grandeur and his gear. . .

Those the determining few—
The precedents, who stay, and still out-last.
There is a residue.
For us
The many-named anonymous
What does it matter that we be
Only the shard, and spoil, and spare,
And whittle, of such statuary?

Francis Meynell

MIRAGE AT MICKLEHAM

This country was not strange to me
Nor quite familiar grown.
I knew it not by stack and tree,
Only by wood and down.

Dazzled by dappled land and light
And scarce-transparent shadow
I thought I saw that quickening sight—
The field close-set, the men in white—
Cricketers in the meadow.

And yet no batsman takes his guard
No ball is bowled, no hit is heard.

The haze is blown, the yew-tree stirs.
For sign of life I search the sward.
Only white stones, these cricketers—
Only white stones in the churchyard.

Francis Meynell

EUCLID ALONE

Euclid alone has looked on Beauty bare.
Let all who prate of Beauty hold their peace,
And lay them prone upon the earth and cease
To ponder on themselves, the while they stare
At nothing, intricately drawn nowhere
In shapes of shifting lineage; let geese
Gabble and hiss, but heroes seek release
From dusty bondage into luminous air.
O blinding hour, O holy, terrible day,
When first the shaft into his vision shone
Of light anatomized! Euclid alone
Has looked on Beauty bare. Fortunate they
Who, though once only and then but far away,
Have heard her massive sandal set on stone.

Edna St. Vincent Millay

NOT IN A SILVER CASKET

Not in a silver casket cool with pearls
Or rich with red corundum or with blue,
Locked, and the key withheld, as other girls
Have given their loves, I give my love to you;
Not in a lovers'-knot, not in a ring
Worked in such fashion, and the legend plain—
Semper fidelis, where a secret spring
Kennels a drop of mischief for the brain:
Love in the open hand, no thing but that,
Ungemmed, unhidden, wishing not to hurt,
As one should bring you cowslips in a hat
Swung from the hand, or apples in her skirt,
I bring you, calling out as children do:
"Look what I have!—And these are all for you."

Edna St. Vincent Millay

IF I SHOULD LEARN, IN SOME QUITE CASUAL WAY

If I should learn, in some quite casual way,
That you were gone, not to return again—
Read from the back-page of a paper, say,
Held by a neighbour in a subway train,
How at the corner of this avenue
And such a street (so are the papers filled)
A hurrying man, who happened to be you,
At noon today had happened to be killed,
I should not cry aloud—I could not cry
Aloud, or wring my hands in such a place—
I should but watch the station lights rush by
With a more careful interest on my face;
Or raise my eyes and read with greater care
Where to store furs and how to treat the hair.

Edna St. Vincent Millay

MY CANDLE

My candle burns at both ends;
It will not last the night;
But ah, my foes, and oh, my friends—
It gives a lovely light!

Edna St. Vincent Millay

ON THE TOILET TABLE OF QUEEN MARIE-ANTOINETTE

This was her table, these her trim outspread
Brushes and trays and porcelain cups for red;
Here sate she, while her women tired and curled
The most unhappy head in all the world.

J. B. B. Nichols

THE IMMIGRANT

When Ruth was old
She'd take her children's children on her knee.
They never wearied to be told
Tales of her girlhood in a far country.

For though her eyes grew dim
Men said of her: "Her heart is always young,"
And Boaz, while she spoke to him,
Loved the faint accent of a foreign tongue.

Frank Kendon

THE PARABLE OF THE OLD MEN AND THE YOUNG

So Abram rose, and clave the wood, and went,
And took the fire with him, and a knife.
And as they sojourned both of them together,
Isaac the first-born spake and said, My Father,
Behold the preparations, fire and iron,
But where the lamb for this burnt-offering?
Then Abram bound the youth with belts and straps,
And builded parapets and trenches there,
And stretchèd forth the knife to slay his son.
When lo! an angel called him out of heaven,
Saying, Lay not thy hand upon the lad,
Neither do anything to him. Behold,
A ram, caught in a thicket by its horns;
Offer the Ram of Pride instead of him.
But the old man would not so, but slew his son,—
And half the seed of Europe, one by one.

Wilfred Owen

TREACHERY

You need not pity me. I shall not die,
Though you have held me in your arms some time,
And taken freely, for an hour's delight,
The best I had of love, the best of rhyme.

You bid me, loving you, lay by the thought
Of trampled souls and wild knight-errantry.
—Lightheart I take my lance in hand again,
And in an hour forget you utterly.

You would have filled my days with memories,
Shot the white moonlight with the colour of you:
That every blackbird's song should be a dirge,
And no flower bloom but rosemary and rue.

Still rain lies grey across the fields, and still
Violet and blue the lightning on the sea . . .
And some day, when your face is not so clear,
I shall find lime as sweet as any tree.

So be not flattered, you that flung me by,
Nor pity my "eternity of pain";
Only, when you lie dreaming, be content.
There is one dream I shall not dream again.

Margaret Cole

WHAT IF A MUCH OF A WHICH OF A WIND

what if a much of a which of a wind
gives the truth to summer's lie;
bloodies with dizzying leaves the sun
and yanks immortal stars awry?
Blow king to beggar and queen to seem
(blow friend to fiend: blow space to time)
—when skies are hanged and oceans drowned,
the single secret will still be man

what if a keen of a lean wind flays
screaming hills with sleet and snow:
strangles valleys by ropes of thing
and stifles forests in white ago?
Blow hope to terror; blow seeing to blind
(blow pity to envy and soul to mind)
—whose hearts are mountains, roots are trees,
it's they shall cry hello to the spring

what if a dawn of a doom of a dream
bites this universe in two,
peels forever out of his grave
and sprinkles nowhere with me and you?
Blow soon to never and never to twice
(blow life to isn't: blow death to was)
—all nothing's only our hugest home;
the most who die, the more we live

E. E. Cummings

From SUMMER DAYS

Before we came the moon-soaked dews were here,
Washing the feet of thrushes as they sang.
No sun was up when this May morning rang
With the first meadow-music of the year;
Those birds had quired their lovely-throated thanks
To see last night's pale vapour disappear,
Blown billowing back in broken, smoking banks
Past the new-painted blue pavilion's shade
To the far, lushy confines of a mere.
The sun rose laughing; daisies reached for him;
Dazzling his eyes at the boundary's unscythed rim
They clambered taller than the tall grass blade,
Gold-hearted each, a midget mountaineer.

God's praise, May sweetness: these, before we came,
Were all the morning saw, or held, or heard.
Now we take on the lease from flower and bird,
Assembling here in traffic for a game.
Soon we'll be ready, every man and lad
Tiptoeing, braced how briskly, for the glad
Commencement and the umpire's call of "Play!"
Busy beneath the hot, slow-circling sun,
We'll carry the morning's echo singing on
With its full, gracious flavour, kind and clear,
Down to the wicket-drawing close of day.

Oh, not alone the birds and flowers had lease
Of these green acres, sweet with grass-born scent,
All centred in a groundsman's popping crease.
Even as we pitch our wicket, flickering near
Are shades of men who found this cricket dear,
And sealed their happy ventures ere we came.

                                          Thomas Moult

LOST LOVE

His eyes are quickened so with grief,
He can watch a grass or leaf
Every instant grow; he can
Clearly through a flint wall see,
Or watch the startled spirit flee
From the throat of a dead man.

Across two counties he can hear
And catch your words before you speak.
The woodlouse or the maggot's weak
Clamour rings in his sad ear,
And noise so slight it would surpass
Credence—drinking sound of grass,
Worm talk, clashing jaws of moth
Chumbling holes in cloth;
The groan of ants who undertake
Gigantic loads for honour's sake,
(Their sinews creak, their breath comes thin);
Whir of spiders when they spin,
And minute whispering, mumbling, sighs
Of idle grubs and flies.

This man is quickened so with grief,
He wanders god-like or like thief
Inside and out, below, above,
Without relief seeking lost love.

Robert Graves

IN TIME

In time all undertakings are made good,
All cruelties remedied,
Each bond resealed more firmly than before—
Befriend us, Time, Love's gaunt executor!

Robert Graves

SHE IS NO LIAR

She is no liar, yet she will wash away
Honey from her lips, blood from her shadowy hand,
And, dressed at dawn in clean white robes will say,
Trusting the ignorant world to understand:
"Such things no longer are; this is today."

Robert Graves

AT BEST, POETS

Woman with her forests, moons, flowers, waters,
And watchful fingers:
We claim no magic comparable to hers—
At best, poets; at worst, sorcerers.

Robert Graves

HEARING, I SAW
For M.C. playing

Hearing, I saw: I saw the hours unfolding,
I saw them flame and die like falling stars,
I saw the shadow of the flesh withholding
The key to life beyond the prison bars.
Hearing, I saw: I saw the earth's abasement,
The poor necessities that chain and bind,
That draw the veil of self across the casement

Obscuring the clear vision of the mind.
Hearing, I saw: I saw cool wisdom seated
Beyond the clamorous tumult of the clay,
I saw the pattern perfectly completed,
I saw all meaning dawn from disarray.
Hearing, I saw. But with your last dark chord,
Beheld the heart defenceless, and the sword.

P. D. Cummins

THE MATRON-CAT'S SONG

So once again the trouble's o'er
And here I sit and sing;
Forgetful of my paramour
And the pickle I was in;
Lord, lord, it is a trying time
We bear when we're expecting,
When folk reproach us for the crime
And frown with glance correcting.
So purra wurra, purra wurra, pronkum pronkum;
Purra wurra pronkum, pronkum purr.

How much I feared my kits would be
Slain in the hour of birth!
And so I sought a sanctuary
Which causes me some mirth;
The surly cook, who hates all cats,
Hath here a little closet,
And here we nest among her hats—
Lord save me when she knows it!
Hey purra wurra, purra wurra, pronkum pronkum;
Purra wurra pronkum, pronkum purr.

Four kits have I of aspect fair,
Though usually but three;
Two female tabs, a charming pair,
Who much resemble me;
Lord, lord, to think upon the sport
Which doth await the hussies,
They'll be no better than they ought
Nor worse than other pussies.
O purra wurra, purra wurra, pronkum pronkum;
Purra wurra pronkum, pronkum purr.

Yet as becomes a mother fond
I dote upon my boys,
And think they will excel beyond
All other toms in noise;
How harsh their manly pelts will be,
How stern and fixed each feature—
If they escape that cruelty
Which man doth work on nature!
Ah purra wurra, purra wurra, pronkum pronkum;
Purra wurra pronkum, pronkum purr.

Those eyes which now are sealèd fast
Nine days against the light
Shall ere few months are overpast
Like stars illume the night;
Those voices that with feeble squall
Demand my whole attention,
Shall earn with rousing caterwaul
Dishonourable mention.
Then purra wurra, purra wurra, pronkum pronkum;
Purra wurra pronkum, pronkum purr.

But then, alas, I shall not care
How flighty they may be,
For ere they're grown I'll have to bear
Another four, or three;
And after all, they are the best
While the whole crew reposes
With fast-shut eyes, weak limbs at rest,
And little wrinkled noses.
So purra wurra, purra wurra, pronkum pronkum;
Purra wurra pronkum, pronkum ryestraw;
Pronkum ryestraw, pronkum ryestraw,
Pur-ra—wur-ra—pron-kum
Pronk . . . Foof. (She sleeps.)

Ruth Pitter

THE SEED SHOP

Here in a quiet and dusty room they lie,
Faded as crumbled stone or shifting sand,
Forlorn as ashes, shrivelled, scentless, dry—
Meadows and gardens running through my hand.

In this brown husk a dale of hawthorn dreams,
A cedar in this narrow cell is thrust
That will drink deeply of a century's streams,
These lilies shall make summer on my dust.

Here in their safe and simple house of death,
Sealed in their shells a million roses leap;
Here I can blow a garden with my breath,
And in my hand a forest lies asleep.

Muriel Stuart

BISHOP SPANIEL'S SERMONS

'Tis more than Spaniel's place is worth
To speak his masters ill:
As long as there is Peace on Earth
He teaches men goodwill.

But when the shells begin to fly
He calls our quarrel just
And bids us keep our powder dry
And place our God in trust.

Colin Ellis

AGAINST PUBLISHING SATIRES

I made an armament to overcome
The embattled brutishness of Tweedledum,
Only to find that weapons forged by me
Upheld the brutish cause of Tweedledee.

Colin Ellis

BYWAY IN BIOGRAPHY

Alfred de Musset
Used to call his cat Pusset.
His accent was affected.
That was to be expected.

Maurice Hare

FREE-WILL AND PREDESTINATION

There was a young man who said "Damn!
It appears to me now that I am
Just a being that moves
In predestinate grooves—
Not a bus, not a bus, but a tram."

Maurice Hare

NOW THAT I AM CLEAN AGAIN
(An escaped prisoner in the American Civil War.)

Now that I am clean again,
Now I've slept and fed,
How shall I remember when
I was someone dead?

Now the balm has worked its art
And the gashes dry,
And the lizard at my heart
Has a sleepy eye,

How shall I remember yet
Freezing underground,
With the wakened lizard set
To the living wound?

Do not ponder the offence
Nor reject the sore,
Do not tear the cerements
Flesh may need once more.

Cold comes back and pain comes back
And the lizard, too.
And the burden in the sack
May be meant for you.

Do not play the risen dunce
With unrisen men.
Lazarus was risen once
But earth gaped again.

Stephen Vincent Benét

19—B.H.

THE WRUNG HEART
On the battle-field

Here is no tryst for love
in these trees of splintered bone.
In this dark wind of pain
wounding the wintry sky,
no love. Let love go by.
Let the wrung heart be stone.
In a lull of the guns
a robin singing I heard;
and when the guns roared again
I saw by his pulsing breast
that he sang on with no rest.
Love has the heart of a bird.

Jack Lindsay

THESE FAITHFUL VERSES

These faithful verses play a double part,
for when the long frustration has relented,
they are the springs that well up in my heart
and flow at last and leave me then contented.
And in a sort they mend my poverty,
who would not be an empty-handed lover,
since they may borrow of their destiny
when richer offerings are faded over.
For, O my love, as I am rich in pain,
whereof this lovers' currency is minted,
so shall my passion's homage yet remain,
alternate pain and song and neither stinted:
and thus my sum of tribute shall increase
in taking both my pain and its release.

Richard Elwes

THE PORCUPINE

Any hound a porcupine nudges
Can't be blamed for harbouring grudges.
I know one hound that laughed all winter
At a porcupine that sat on a splinter.

Ogden Nash

THE LION

Oh, weep for Mr and Mrs Bryan!
He was eaten by a lion;
Following which, the lion's lioness
Up and swallowed Bryan's Bryaness.

Ogden Nash

ANOTHER TIME

For us like any other fugitive,
Like the numberless flowers that cannot number
And all the beasts that need not remember,
It is today in which we live.

So many try to say Not Now,
So many have forgotten how
To say I Am, and would be
Lost, if they could, in history.

Bowing, for instance, with such old-world grace
To a proper flag in a proper place,
Muttering like ancients as they stump upstairs
Of Mine and His or Ours and Theirs.

Just as if time were what they used to will
When it was gifted with possession still,
Just as if they were wrong
In no more wishing to belong.

No wonder then so many die of grief,
So many are so lonely as they die;
No one has yet believed or liked a lie,
Another time has other lives to live.

W. H. Auden

LUCIFER

Lucifer did not wish to murder God,
But only to reduce His Self-esteem.
Weary of brightness where no shadow showed,
What took the rebel's fancy was a dream

Of God bewildered, angered out of measure
And driven, almost weeping, to implore,
"I built this Heaven for My Angels' pleasure,
And yet you like it not. What would you more?"

At this, of course, with most Divine compassion,
Lucifer, all forgiving and adept,
Would soon have taught his Master how to fashion
A Heaven such as angels could accept.

Norman Cameron

HUNTER TRIALS

It's awf'lly bad luck on Diana,
Her ponies have swallowed their bits;
She fished down their throats with a spanner
And frightened them all into fits.

So now she's attempting to borrow.
Do lend her some bits, Mummy, *do*;
I'll lend her my own for to-morrow,
But to-day *I*'ll be wanting them too.

Just look at Prunella on Guzzle,
The wizardest pony on earth;
Why doesn't she slacken his muzzle
And tighten the breech in his girth?

I say, Mummy, there's Mrs Geyser
And doesn't she look pretty sick?
I bet it's because Mona Lisa
Was hit on the hock with a brick.

Miss Blewitt says Monica threw it,
But Monica says it was Joan,
And Joan's very thick with Miss Blewitt,
So Monica's sulking alone.

And Margaret failed in her paces,
Her withers got tied in a noose,
So her coronet's caught in the traces
And now all her fetlocks are loose.

Oh, it's me now. I'm terribly nervous.
I wonder if Smudges will shy.
She's practically certain to swerve as
Her Pelham is over one eye.

★ ★ ★

Oh, wasn't it naughty of Smudges?
Oh, Mummy, I'm sick with disgust.
She threw me in front of the Judges,
And my silly old collarbone's bust.

John Betjeman

SONG

There is no joy in water apart from the sun,
There is no beauty not emphasized by death,
No meaning in home if exile were unknown;
A man who lives in a thermostat lives beneath
A bell of glass alone with the smell of death.

There is no beauty like that seen from a cliff;
The beauty of women comes and goes with a breath;
A man must offer the beauty of his wife
In sacrifice to give his children breath—
The children will walk on their folded hands of
   death.

Nothing in life is near and nothing far
Apart from love; a man can live beneath
His roof more lonely than an outer star;
And know a woman's beauty, a flower's breath
Walking alone in the valley of the shadow of death.

R. N. Currey

MEETING POINT

Time was away and somewhere else,
There were two glasses and two chairs
And two people with the one pulse
(Somebody stopped the moving stairs):
Time was away and somewhere else.

And they were neither up nor down,
The stream's music did not stop
Flowing through heather, limpid brown,
Although they sat in a coffee shop
And they were neither up nor down.

The bell was silent in the air
Holding its inverted poise—
Between the clang and clang a flower,
A brazen calyx of no noise:
The bell was silent in the air.

The camels crossed the miles of sand
That stretched around the cups and plates;
The desert was their own, they planned
To portion out the stars and dates:
The camels crossed the miles of sand.

Time was away and somewhere else,
The waiter did not come, the clock
Forgot them and the radio waltz
Came out like water from a rock:
Time was away and somewhere else.

Her fingers flicked away the ash
That bloomed again in tropic trees:
Not caring if the markets crash
When they had forests such as these,
Her fingers flicked away the ash.

God or whatever means the Good
Be praised that time can stop like this,
That what the heart has understood
Can verify in the body's peace
God or whatever means the Good.

Time was away and she was here
And life no longer what it was,
The bell was silent in the air
And all the room a glow because
Time was away and she was here.

Louis MacNeice

THE SUNLIGHT ON THE GARDEN

The sunlight on the garden
Hardens and grows cold,
We cannot cage the minute
Within its nets of gold,
When all is told
We cannot beg for pardon.

Our freedom as free lances
Advances towards its end;
The earth compels, upon it
Sonnets and birds descend;
And soon, my friend,
We shall have no time for dances.

The sky was good for flying
Defying the church bells
And every evil iron
Siren and what it tells:
The earth compels,
We are dying, Egypt, dying

And not expecting pardon,
Hardened in heart anew,
But glad to have sat under
Thunder and rain with you,
And grateful too
For sunlight on the garden.

Louis MacNeice

WINTER ACONITES

Small as a breath, so drawn together,
A people, not a flower;
As if they made their heart's own weather
From the heart's warmer power,

They live: and neither blame the land
That bears them, nor their birth.
Nearest to earth, they understand
The nature of the earth.

For while branch-fingered winter here
Fastens us to our room,
They take the coldest of the year
And build in it their home.

Robert Gittings

THE BLIND YOUTH

My world was night
Until He came.
The sun's light
And the fire's flame

Warmly spoke
To this wall of skin,
Yet never woke
The fires within.

Faces were voices,
Moving lips,
Hollows and spaces
For finger-tips;

But something under
Each fluttering lid
Told of the wonder
My darkness hid:

And as I lay
By the Gate and clutched
The bowl one day,
My lids were touched.

I thought, by his feeling,
That he was blind,
Those hands revealing
The touch-quick mind.

I felt my eyes,
Where his fingers lay,
Stir and rise
With the hardening clay;

And when I stooped
To wash it away,
In the water I scooped
The day was day!

The pool, it broke
Like a bowl of dye—
Unsolid, a-soak
With the autumn sky.

Sunlight talking,
Branches tossing,
The man walking,
His two legs crossing . . .

That's all my story:
Set me free.
The world is glory,
And I can see!

Clive Sansom

SONNET TO MY MOTHER

Most near, most dear, most loved and most far,
Under the window where I often found her
Sitting as huge as Asia, seismic with laughter,
Gin and chicken helpless in her Irish hand,
Irresistible as Rabelais but most tender for
The lame dogs and hurt birds that surround her,—
She is a procession no one can follow after
But be like a little dog following a brass band.
She will not glance up at the bomber nor condescend
To drop her gin and scuttle to a cellar,
But lean on the mahogany table like a mountain
Whom only faith can move, and so I send
O all my faith and all my love to tell her
That she will move from mourning into morning.

George Barker

COME CAROL, MAKE CAROL

Come carol, make carol,
Low, oxen and kine,
For a cave's candle glimmer,
A planet's clear shine.

The hill sheep are folded
Together for warm,
The shepherds sing softly
To tell there's no harm.

Come carol, make carol,
Low, oxen, sound, ass,
For the daughter of David,
And time come to pass.

A star in the heavens,
There is peace for a day,
The nations are friendly,
The kings on the way.

Come carol, make carol,
Low, oxen and kine,
For the daughter of David,
The promise and sign.

Her spouse has asked urgently
Room at the inn,
But the answer is No
Midst festivity's din.

Come carol, make carol,
Low, oxen, sound, ass,
For the miracle due
Of Humility's Glass.

The angels expectant
Stand silent in sky,
And the shepherds are glad
Without knowing why.

Come carol, make carol,
Low, oxen and kine,
For the daughter of David
And her Infant Divine.

C. C. Gould

CAROL ON CORFU

I, per se I, I sing on.
Let flesh falter, or let bone break
Break, yet the salt of a poem holds on,
Even in empty weather
When beak and feather have done.

I am such fiddle-glib strokes,
As play on the nerves, glance the bare bone
With the madman's verve I quicken,
Leaven and liven body's prime carbon,
I, per se I, alone.

This is my medicine: trees speak and doves
Talk, woods walk: in the pith of the planet
Is undertone, overtone, status of music: God
Opens each fent, scent, memory, aftermath
In the sky and the sod.

O per se O, I sing on.
Never tongue falters or love lessens,
Lessens. The salt of the poem lives on
Like this carol of empty weather
Now feather and beak have gone.

Lawrence Durrell

AND DEATH SHALL HAVE NO DOMINION

And death shall have no dominion.
Dead men naked they shall be one
With the man in the wind and the west moon;
When their bones are picked clean and the clean
   bones gone,
They shall have stars at elbow and foot;

Though they go mad they shall be sane,
Though they sink through the sea they shall rise
   again;
Though lovers be lost love shall not;
And death shall have no dominion.

And death shall have no dominion.
Under the windings of the sea
They lying long shall not die windily;
Twisting on racks when sinews give way,
Strapped to a wheel, yet they shall not break;
Faith in their hands shall snap in two,
And the unicorn evils run them through;
Split all ends up they shan't crack;
And death shall have no dominion.

And death shall have no dominion.
No more may gulls cry at their ears
Or waves break loud on the seashores;
Where blew a flower may a flower no more
Lift its head to the blows of the rain;
Though they be mad and dead as nails,
Heads of the characters hammer through daisies;
Break in the sun till the sun breaks down,
And death shall have no dominion.

Dylan Thomas

THE HAND THAT SIGNED THE PAPER
FELLED A CITY

The hand that signed the paper felled a city;
Five sovereign fingers taxed the breath,
Doubled the globe of dead and halved a country;
These five kings did a king to death.

The mighty hand leads to a sloping shoulder,
The finger joints are cramped with chalk;
A goose's quill has put an end to murder
That put an end to talk.

The hand that signed the treaty bred a fever,
And famine grew, and locusts came;
Great is the hand that holds dominion over
Man by a scribbled name.

The five kings count the dead but do not soften
The crusted wound nor pat the brow;
A hand rules pity as a hand rules heaven;
Hands have no tears to flow.

Dylan Thomas

WATER MUSIC

Deep in the heart of the lake
Where the last light is clinging
A strange foreboding voice
Is patiently singing.

Do not fear to venture
Where the last light trembles
Because you were in love.
Love never dissembles.

Fear no more the boast, the bully,
The lies, the vain labour.
Make no show for death
As for a rich neighbour.

What stays of the great religions?
An old priest, an old birth.
What stays of the great battles?
Dust on the earth.

Cold is the lake water
And dark as history.
Hurry not and fear not
This oldest mystery.

This strange voice singing,
This slow deep drag of the lake,
This yearning, yearning, this ending
Of the heart and its ache.

Alun Lewis

KEATS AT TEIGNMOUTH: 1818
(*Three years before his death*)

By the wild sea-wall I wandered
Blinded by the salting sun,
While the sulky Channel thundered
Like an old Trafalgar gun.

And I watched the gaudy river
Under trees of lemon-green,
Coiling like a scarlet bugle
Through the valley of the Teign.

When spring fired her fusilladoes
Salt-spray, sea-spray on the sill,
When the budding scarf of April
Ravelled on the Devon hill,

Then I saw the crystal poet
Leaning on the old sea-rail;
In his breast lay death, the lover,
In his head, the nightingale.

Charles Causley

TYWATER

Death of Sir Nihil, book the *nth*,
Upon the charred and clotted sward,
Lacking the lily of our Lord,
Alases of the hyacinth.

Could flicker from behind his ear
A whistling silver throwing knife
And with a holler punch the life
Out of a swallow in the air.

Behind the lariat's butterfly
Shuttled his white and gritted grin,
And cuts of sky would roll within
The noose-hole, when he spun it high.

The violent, neat and practised skill
Was all he loved and all he learned;
When he was hit, his body turned
To clumsy dirt before it fell.

And what to say of him, God knows.
Such violence. And such repose.

Richard Wilbur

WAR POET

I am the man who looked for peace and found
My own eyes barbed.
I am the man who groped for words and found
An arrow in my hand.
I am the builder whose firm walls surround
A slipping land.
When I grow sick or mad
Mock me not nor chain me:
When I reach for the wind
Cast me not down:
Though my face is a burnt book
And a wasted town.

Sidney Keyes

FIRST SIGHT

Lambs that learn to walk in snow
When their bleating clouds the air
Meet a vast unwelcome, know
Nothing but a sunless glare.
Newly stumbling to and fro
All they find, outside the fold,
Is a wretched width of cold.

As they wait beside the ewe,
Her fleeces wetly caked, there lies
Hidden round them, waiting too,
Earth's immeasurable surprise.
They could not grasp it if they knew,
What so soon will wake and grow
Utterly unlike the snow.

Philip Larkin

THE PHOENIX

As great as earth with child or sun with fire, the
    dawn
Of his life breaks. Annunciation cancels the cold
Nest of ashes where he lies dead. Now the winged
    spawn
Of love's hot mystery grows young while we grow
    old.
If sudden or slow agony, if sleep or pain
Find out the fire, choke the source and drown the
    man
Then in that limp shell may the busy princess reign,
May the bee suck and the slow sun kindle another
    man.
In the heart's red image of feast and flame
The cool, arterial wine rots in the house of his name.

As busily as stars gnawing the hot heart of heaven
He pecks his grave, greedy again to be born.
Cold ashes that were his death are now his leaven
Raising the flesh once more to bleed upon a thorn
And share his limbs into the infinite mouth
Of human kind to feed the hunger of that fire
Where spirit melts and merges into the hazardous
    truth
And man and God burn with one desire.
Love's gain and loss, the heavy claims of earth,
The mortgage of all living kind cannot escape his
    birth.

With one desire heart breaks and angels fall,
God dies and man corrupts: who knows the remedy?

The stars recede, the elements increase, and small
And weak as grass we and our citadels decay.
As we prosper something dies without a cry,
A child that chokes in the womb; unseen calamities
That haunt the docks and derricks, the rich quay,
The markets, factories, all monuments of avarice.
Trading among the continents the cunning Ulysses
Grows rich while elsewhere he, the willing soldier,
    dies.

Ambiguous the dead to live again, the living to live
On dying: who can puzzle it? And yet our lips
Without horror his flesh and blood gladly receive.
Bearing him to distant war go the grey ships.
Money like rain slakes the parched roots of the state
And metal magnifies the glory of man's fear and
    greed.
Who rises from the city planted with our hate?
Who rises from the ashes, who on ashes feed?
Who dares to venture in the mortal flame
And bear once more the torture of man's name?

Richard Selig

GHOSTS

Those houses haunt in which we leave
Something undone. It is not those
Great words or silences of love

That spread their echoes through a place
And fill the locked-up unbreathed gloom.
Ghosts do not haunt with any face

That we have known; they only come
With arrogance to thrust at us
Our own omissions in a room.

The words we would not speak they use,
The deeds we dared not act they flaunt,
Our nervous silences they bruise;

It is our helplessness they choose
And our refusals that they haunt.

Elizabeth Jennings

SECOND YEAR IN A SEMINARY

We have a past in common now
week after week of blue and green,
the handled pages of school-books,
the eye forgets what it had seen,
observes without observing how
the landscape alters while it looks.

Birds in the dawn building the day
in the long sweet between-seasons
draw colour from the trees and sky
yellow and green, crimson and bronze,
the colours have dissolved away
and things are in their last beauty.

The finished books drop out of mind,
we test for winter, balancing
purple with pink, sky with the ground,
and the ground-mist with everything
that analytic sight can find
or the life-loving sense has found.

We are alone and everyone
exists in his own idleness:
each rousing from a sluggish bed
the trailing dawn the dawn's slowness
and a few traces of the sun
to growths of light inside the head.

Colours and light mark what we know,
the face and gesture stay the same,
at winter dusk observing how
the pink was dwindling while it came
too cold for anything to grow,
we have a past in common now.

                                          Peter Levi, S.J.

THE FINAL WORD

Since I was ten I have not been unkind
To anyone save those who were most close:
Of my close friends one of the best is blind,
One deaf, and one a priest who can't write prose.
None has a quiet mind.

Deep into night my friends with tired faces
Break language up for one word to remain,
The tall forgiving word nothing effaces,
Though without maps it travel, and explain
A pure truth in all places.

Yet death, if it should fall on us, would be
Only the smallest settling into beds:
Our last words lost because Eternity
Made its loud noise above our lifted heads
Before we ceased to see.

But, all made blind and deaf, the final word
Bequeathed by us, at the far side of
Experience, waits: there neither man nor bird
Settles, except with knowledge, or much love.
There Adam's voice is heard.

And my true love, a skylark in each eye,
Walks the small grass, and the small frightened
   things
Scurry to her for comfort, and can't die
While she still lives, and all the broken Kings
Kneel to her and know why.

Because she turns, her love at last expressed,
Into my arms: and then I cannot die.
I have furnished my heart to be her nest
For even if at dusk she choose to fly
Afterwards she must rest.

Dom Moraes

CAINSMORNING

Having eliminated his dear brother
He let tears fall and wandered off alone,
Blaming himself in whispers for another
Error, yet knowing that he could not atone:

"In this day's silence I am unattended,
Yet (understand me) I did all for good:
Though I am sorry now that I have ended
My thirst for freedom in my brother's blood."

The morning changed, grew chilly and transparent.
Suddenly all the light shrank and was gone:
And then at last his guilt became apparent
Even to him, yet he went slowly on.

The mountains sneered, the river whispered Slayer!
He felt a saraband start in his brain,
And turned his face to heaven, and saw his prayer
Melt in the cold, the grey, the faceless rain.

Dom Moraes

LANDSCAPE

The wind blows. Winds blow the
Hill green and grey. Olives
Are alive with light. Fat grow the
Grapes green misted with a mist that lives.

I wait living with these things by the lake.
My eyelids poise over my eyes. Closing
To kill sight they hover in the wake
Of the crowd of things their uncovering unclosed.

Where over the lake two hawks poise and hover.
Intention tips their wings like light.
When the wake of the boat uncovers
Fish tossed out dead they arch their flight.

Robert Wells

INDEX OF POETS

Including dates of birth and death and titles of poems. Where a poem was untitled, the first line is given in italics.

21 + B.H.

INDEX OF TITLES AND FIRST LINES

Where the title is an abbreviated first line, it is not listed separately.

ACKNOWLEDGMENTS

The Editor's task has been made more pleasurable by the help of Pamela Zander. His thanks are due also to Margaret Clark; and to the following for permission to reprint copyright material: Faber & Faber Ltd and Random House, Inc. for "Another Time" from COLLECTED SHORTER POEMS by W. H. *Auden* and THE COLLECTED POETRY OF W. H. AUDEN, copyright 1945 by W. H. Auden;

Faber & Faber Ltd and October House Inc. for "Sonnet to My Mother" from COLLECTED POEMS by *George Barker*;

A. D. Peters & Co. for "Auvergnat", "How did the party go in Portman Square" and "The Death and Last Confession of Wandering Peter" by *Hilaire Belloc*;

the estate of the late Stephen Vincent Benét for "Now that I am clean again" from JOHN BROWN'S BODY by *Stephen Vincent Benét*, copyright 1927, 1928 by S. V. Benét, copyright renewed 1955, 1956 by Rosemary Carr Benét;

John Murray Ltd for "Hunter Trials" from A FEW LATE CHRYS-ANTHEMUMS by *John Betjeman*;

the Clarendon Press, Oxford, for "I heard a linnet courting", "I love all beauteous things" and "The idle life I lead" by *Robert Bridges*;

Sidgwick & Jackson Ltd for "Heaven" and "The Busy Heart" by *Rupert Brooke*;

the Hogarth Press Ltd for "Lucifer" by *Norman Cameron*;

David Higham Associates Ltd for "Keats at Teignmouth" from UNION STREET by *Charles Causley*, published by Rupert Hart-Davis Ltd;

Basil Blackwell & Mott Ltd for "Noah and the Rabbit" by *Hugh Chesterman*;

Miss D. E. Collins and J. M. Dent & Sons Ltd for "The Donkey" and "The Praise of Dust" from A WILD KNIGHT AND OTHER POEMS by *G. K. Chesterton*;

Mrs Margaret Cole for her poem "Treachery";

the Cresset Press for "The Country Bedroom" and "The Old Servant" by *Frances Cornford*;

Faber & Faber Ltd for "what if a much of a which of a wind" from SELECTED POEMS by *E. E. Cummings*, and Harcourt, Brace &

Thomas Moult for his poem "Summer Days";

Faber & Faber Ltd for "The Return" from COLLECTED POEMS by *Edwin Muir;*

J. M. Dent & Sons Ltd and Curtis Brown Ltd for "The Porcupine" and "The Lion" by *Ogden Nash*;

Captain Francis Newbolt for "Drake's Drum" from POEMS NEW AND OLD by *Sir Henry Newbolt*, published by John Murray Ltd;

John Murray Ltd for "Cats and Kings" from COLLECTED POEMS by *Alfred Noyes*;

Sir Frederic J. Osborn for his poem "There is a Time";

Chatto and Windus Ltd and New Directions, New York, for "The Parable of the Old Men and the Young" from COLLECTED POEMS by *Wilfred Owen*, copyright © Chatto & Windus Ltd, 1963;

the Cresset Press for "The Matron-Cat's Song" by *Ruth Pitter*;

the author and New Directions, New York, for "Envoi (1919)" from PERSONAE by *Ezra Pound*, copyright 1926, 1954 by Ezra Pound;

Simon de Robinet Raleigh for "Wishes at a Garden Party" by *Walter Raleigh*;

David Higham Associates Ltd for "The Blind Youth" from THE WITNESS AND OTHER POEMS by *Clive Sansom*, published by Methuen & Co. Ltd;

Siegfried Sassoon for his poems "A Prayer to Time", "Base Details" and "To an Old Lady Dead";

the Dolmen Press Ltd for "The Phoenix" by *Richard Selig*;

David Higham Associates Ltd for "The Little Ghost who Died for Love" from COLLECTED POEMS OLD AND NEW by *Dame Edith Sitwell*, published by Faber & Faber Ltd;

Mrs Iris Wise, Macmillan & Co. Ltd, London, the Macmillan Company of Canada Ltd and the Macmillan Company of New York for "In the Cool of the Evening" and "The Fulness of Time" from COLLECTED POEMS by *James Stephens*, copyright 1912 by the Macmillan Company, renewed 1940 by James Stephens, "What Tomas said in a pub" from COLLECTED POEMS by *James Stephens*, copyright 1909 by the Macmillan Company, "The Wood of Flowers" from COLLECTED POEMS by *James Stephens*, copyright 1915 by the Macmillan Company, renewed 1943 by James Stephens, and "Little Things" from A POETRY RECITAL by *James*